· T R O P H I E S ·

Practice Book

Grade 2 ◆ Volume Two

Harcourt

Orlando   Boston   Dallas   Chicago   San Diego

Visit The Learning Site!

www.harcourtschool.com

Printed in the United States of America

ISBN 13: 978-0-15-323511-5   ISBN 10: 0-15-323511-X

30 31 32 33 0982 13 12 11 10

Contents

BANNER DAYS

Name _____

▶ **Write the words where they belong in the chart.**

how	crown	out	brow	around
mouth	now	house	found	clown

<u>c</u>ow

m<u>ou</u>se

cow	mouse
how	house
crown	around
broun	found
clown	mouth
how	out

SCHOOL-HOME CONNECTION Work with your child to think of a sentence using both an *ou* word and an *ow* word, such as *There's a clown in my house.*

1

Practice Book
Banner Days

Name _____

▶ **Read the Spelling Words. Sort the words
and write them where they belong.**

**Spelling
Words**

Words with *ou*	
1. _____	6. _____
2. _____	7. _____
3. _____	**Words with *ow***
4. _____	8. _____
5. _____	9. _____
	10. _____

how
mouth
out
house
without
found
around
sound
now
brow
beauties
skies
started
mean
cow

▶ **Sort the words that are left by the number
of syllables.**

One-Syllable Words	Two-Syllable Words
11. _____	14. _____
12. _____	15. _____
13. _____	

Name _____

▶ **Solve the riddles. Write a word from the box on each line.**

round	house	mouth	crown	frown
clowns	without	cow	brow	sound

1. People live in this. It's a _____.

2. This animal says "moo." It's a _____.

3. This is not with. It's _____.

4. A king wears this on his head.

   It's a _____.

5. This is not a smile.

   It's a _____.

6. When you hear something, you hear this.

   It's a _____.

7. This is the shape of a circle. It's _____.

8. You talk with this. It's your _____.

9. These funny people are in a circus.

   They are _____.

SCHOOL-HOME CONNECTION Ask your child
to draw and label a picture for one of the words
used on this page. Then ask him or her to point
out the letters that stand for the vowel sound.

3

Practice Book
Banner Days

Name _____

▶ **Finish the story. On each line, write a word from the shirts.**

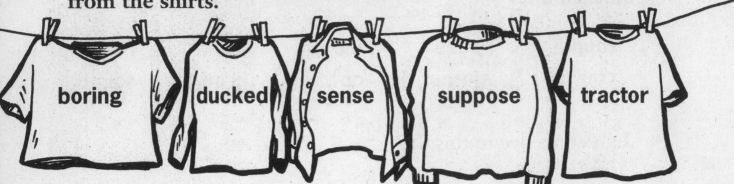

boring   ducked   sense   suppose   tractor

I _____ Grandpa lives in the best place in the

world. It's never _____ on his farm. It's fun to ride on

grandpa's _____. One cold day I _____

under the barnyard fence and saw all the animals sleeping together.

I guess it made _____ for the animals to sleep together to

keep warm.

 TRY THIS! Write a story about your favorite farm animal. Use as many Vocabulary Words as you can.

Practice Book
Banner Days

Name _____

Skill Reminder • **A pronoun takes the place of a
noun. *I*, *you*, *he*, *she*, *it*, and *they* are pronouns.**

▶ Finish each sentence. Write a pronoun from the box that can
take the place of the noun in ( ). Remember to begin each
sentence with a capital letter.

I	you	he	she	they	it

1. _____ went to the farm. **(Max)**

2. _____ went, too. **(Liz)**

3. _____ saw many farm
animals. **(the children)**

4. _____ were in the barn. **(the horses)**

5. _____ asked about the snake. **(Mr. Jung)**

6. _____ did not live on the farm. **(the snake)**

7. Mrs. Grant said, "_____ liked that snake." **(Mrs. Grant)**

8. Mrs. Grant told Angie, "_____ would have liked
it, too." **(Angie)**

TRY THIS! Draw a picture of something you and your friends like to
do. Write two sentences to go with your picture. Use the
pronouns *I* and *we* in your sentences.

© Harcourt

Practice Book
Banner Days

| **Syllable Rule** | • **When a two-syllable word has an ending, it is usually divided between the base word and the ending. Example: fear/less wish/ful** |

▶ **On the line write the boldfaced word in syllables. Remember not to divide one-syllable words.**

1. Rocky has ————————— days.
      cheerful

2. He barks ————————— when the doorbell rings.
      louder

3. He ————————— catch with me yesterday.
      played

4. Rocky ————————— takes long walks with me.
      gladly

5. He never ————————— my shoes.
      eats

6. Rocky is ————————— when he plays.
      careful

Name _____

▶ **Read the story. Then complete the sentences.**

The Rainy Day

It was a rainy day at school. We could not play outside. The playground was soaked. After lunch, we walked back to the classroom. There we saw markers, paints, and crayons on our desks. Our teacher smiled. It was time for arts and crafts. Everyone was excited.

1. The children could not play outside because

_____

_____.

> 💡 **Tip**
> A cause is why something happened.

2. Everyone was excited because

_____

_____.

> 💡 **Tip**
> An effect can often be found just before the cause.

© Harcourt

SCHOOL-HOME CONNECTION With your child, read a newspaper article. Help your child figure out a cause and an effect of the event described.

7

Practice Book
Banner Days

Name _____

▶ **Read the story. On each line below, write the
underlined word and add the correct suffix.**

Everyone was happy. It was a **(1)** joy day. It
was sunny. The skies were blue and
(2) cloud. The second grade was
planting a garden. "Pay attention,"
said their teacher, Mrs. Dell. "Be
(3) care." The children each
buried a **(4)** hand of carrot seeds in
the dirt. They had lots of carrots to use
in carrot cake and carrot soup and carrot salad. One day a
(5) sound visitor stole into their garden. It was a rabbit. The
children watched the rabbit eat a **(6)** mouth of carrots.

1. _____   2. _____

3. _____   4. _____

5. _____   6. _____

SCHOOL-HOME CONNECTION With your child,
make up sentences with words that end with –ful
or –less, such as *truthful, careful, nameless* or
timeless. Talk about the base words: *truth, care,
name, time.* Ask your child how the ending –ful or –less
changes the meaning of the base word.

8

Practice Book
Banner Days

Name _____

▶ **Circle the best answer to each riddle.**

1. This is not rough.   soap   smooth   smock   smile

2. You sweep with this.   broad   broke   broom   born

3. They grow under trees.   roots   rope   road   role

4. This shines in the
   night sky.   moon   mom   mode   mouse

5. You eat this.   fool   foam   foot   food

6. This is a kind of
   TV show.   car   tune   cartoon   croon

7. This has two wheels,
   and you stand on it.   spring   sight   scooter   school

8. This is the top part
   of a house.   read   rule   rope   roof

9. This is like a shoe.   boot   baby   book   box

10. You eat soup with this.   spool   sport   spot   spoon

© Harcourt

SCHOOL-HOME CONNECTION With your child, look around the house and write down all the words containing *oo* for things you find.

9

Practice Book
Banner Days

Name _____

▶ **Finish the story. On each line, write a word from the box.**

coin	boy	toy	cowboys
soil	point	join	

A Day to Enjoy

One day a **(1)** _____ named

Jack was digging in the **(2)** _____ .

He found a shiny **(3)** _____ .
Jack knew what he wanted to do. "Mom, may we go

to the **(4)** _____ store?" he asked. "Yes,
Jack," said Mom. "Let's ask your dad to

(5) _____ us." At the store, Jack found
what he was looking for. It was on a high shelf. He had to

(6) _____ to what he wanted. The clerk

took it down. She put the two **(7)** _____
and two horses in Jack's hands. What a lucky day it had been
for Jack!

SCHOOL-HOME CONNECTION Show your child several different coins. Have your child name the coins and then think of other words that have the *oi* sound.

© Harcourt

▶ **Read the Spelling Words. Sort the words and write them where they belong.**

Words with *oi*	Words with *oy*
1. _____	7. _____
2. _____	8. _____
3. _____	9. _____
4. _____	10. _____
5. _____	
6. _____	

Spelling Words

voices
cowboys
toy
enjoyment
oil
point
join
soil
joy
coin
around
without
fire
train
wait

▶ **Write the words that are left in alphabetical order.**

11. _____	14. _____
12. _____	15. _____
13. _____	

Name _____

▶ **Solve the riddles. Write a word from the box
on each line.**

| spoil | voices | oil | joy | foil |
| toy | cowboys | soil | point | join |

1. You can grow flowers in this. It's _____.

2. A pencil has one of these. It's a _____.

3. People feel this when they are happy.

   It's _____.

4. This may happen if you leave milk out.

   It may _____.

5. You do this to be part of a team.

   You _____.

6. You may use this when you cook.

   It is _____.

7. When we sing, we use these.

   We use our _____.

8. People wrap food in this. It's _____.

9. A doll is one of these. It's a _____.

10. You may find these men riding horses.

    They are _____.

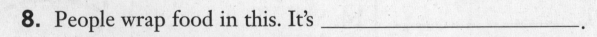**SCHOOL-HOME CONNECTION** Ask your child
to make up riddles for the words *boy* and *boil*.
Have your child write the words and point to the
letters that make the *oi* sound.

12

Practice Book
Banner Days

© Harcourt

Name _____

▶ **Solve the riddles. On each line, write a word from the box.**

captured	imagination	manners	matador
plains	relax	vacation	

1. He waves a cape. Who is he?

He's a _____.

2. If you say "please," what do you have?

You have good _____.

3. If you sit and rest, what do you do?

You _____.

4. You won't see any hills here. Where are you?

You are on the _____.

5. You go on this for fun. What is it?

It's a _____.

6. If you roped a cow, what did you do?

You _____ it.

7. What do you use to think about new things?

You use your _____.

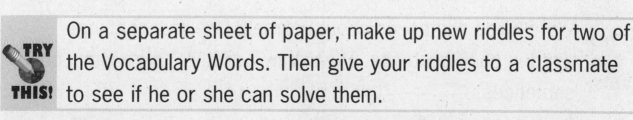

TRY THIS! On a separate sheet of paper, make up new riddles for two of the Vocabulary Words. Then give your riddles to a classmate to see if he or she can solve them.

© Harcourt

Skill Reminder • **A describing word tells about a noun. Some describing words tell about color, size, or shape.**

▶ **Read the words under each line. Choose the describing word. Write it on the line.**

1. I am a _____ cowboy.
   (take   tall   talk)

2. I have a _____ hat.
   (big   bark   bus)

3. I wear _____ boots.
   (by   black   blow)

4. I ride a _____ horse.
   (bird   brown   build)

5. I have a _____ rope.
   (long   lunch   land)

6. I can make a _____ loop with my rope.
   (run   round   race)

7. Those _____ cows are mine.
   (when   white   went)

TRY THIS! Write three sentences about yourself. Use a describing word in each sentence. Then draw a picture to go with your sentences.

© Harcourt

Practice Book
Banner Days

Name _____

How I Spent My
Summer Vacation

Vowel Diphthongs:
/oi/ oi, oy
TEST PREP

▶ **Find the word with the same sound as the underlined letters in the first word. Fill in the circle next to your choice.**

Example j<u>oi</u>n

- ○ toy
- ○ boat
- ○ top

1 c<u>oi</u>n

- ○ crown
- ○ room
- ○ boy

💡 **Tip**
Say the word and listen to the sound that the underlined letters make.

2 enj<u>oy</u>

- ○ corner
- ○ book
- ○ point

3 b<u>oi</u>led

- ○ destroy
- ○ butter
- ○ bother

💡 **Tip**
Ignore any word choices that don't make sense.

© Harcourt

15

▶ **Read the story. Then fill in the chart of causes
and effects.**

I had the day off from school. I was going to play soccer,
but it rained. I stayed at home instead. I decided to give my
dog a bath. We didn't have any dog shampoo, so I washed her
with toothpaste. She seemed pretty clean, but her fur was kind
of sticky. I had to give her another bath with human shampoo.
Now her fur is shiny.

CAUSE	EFFECT
_____ _____	The narrator stayed at home.
There was no dog shampoo.	_____ _____
The dog's fur was sticky.	_____ _____
_____ _____	The dog's fur is shiny.

© Harcourt

SCHOOL-HOME CONNECTION Play a cause-
and-effect game with your child. Ask your child
what he or she would have done today if it had
snowed, been sunny, or rained ice cream. Make
up as many funny effects as you can.

16

Practice Book
Banner Days

Name _____

▶ **Write the words from the box that best complete the poem. Remember that the word you write should rhyme with the last word in the line before.**

| steer | reindeer | cheers | year | hear | beard |

I have a big sled over here.

It gets pulled along by eight _____.

Some people think it's really weird,

But I also have a big white _____.

Want a ride? Have no fear.

I know exactly how to _____.

I drive my sled both far and near,

But I only drive it once a _____.

What's that noise, so loud and clear?

Those are reindeer hooves you _____.

If I can't drive, I shed tears,

But if I can, I yell out _____.

© Harcourt

SCHOOL-HOME CONNECTION With your child,
choose three or four words from this exercise.
Ask your child to see how many words he or she
can think of that rhyme with them.

17

Practice Book
Banner Days

▶ **Circle and write the word that completes each sentence.**

1. My favorite animal is a _____.
green   goose   good

2. My favorite color is _____.
balloon   blue   boys

3. You can see the _____ in the sky at night.
moon   main   mop

4. His sister lost a baby _____.
tune   tree   tooth

5. A detective looked for a _____ to solve his case.
clue   cross   crane

6. There is a bell on the _____ of the school.
rope   roof   rake

7. The cowboy wore his red _____.
boots   branch   bake

8. Mary used _____ to stick her cut outs to her paper.
grade   grass   glue

SCHOOL-HOME CONNECTION With your child, write a letter to someone asking for information on a topic of interest. Have your child include words that contain oo or ue.

18

Practice Book
Banner Days

© Harcourt

▶ **Read the Spelling Words. Sort the words, and write them where they belong.**

Words with *oo*	Words with *ue*
1. _____	6. _____
2. _____	7. _____
3. _____	8. _____
4. _____	9. _____
5. _____	10. _____

Spelling Words

blue
too
glue
zoo
room
clue
due
rooftop
true
noontime
cowboys
voices
letter
sea
won't

▶ **Write the words that are left in alphabetical order.**

11. _____	14. _____
12. _____	15. _____
13. _____	

© Harcourt

19

Name _____

▶ **Circle and write the word that completes each sentence.**

1. I mailed my letter at _____.

   noon   note   noise

2. Are whales really _____?

   blue   blow   blade

3. I want to know if that story is _____.

   tree   true   try

4. I will ask the man at the _____.

   zip   zero   zoo

5. I hope he sends me a _____.

   coal   clue   coil

6. My library book about whales is _____.

   dry   drop   due

7. I need to hurry home to my _____.

   ramp   room   roam

8. I have to finish my book _____.

   seen   shine   soon

9. I am so close to home that I can see the top of my

   _____.

   ray   roof   raft

SCHOOL-HOME CONNECTION Have your child list the words from the lesson that have the ōō sound spelled oo as in moon. Then ask your child to list the words that have the ōō sound spelled ue as in blue.

20

Practice Book
Banner Days

▶ **Complete the labels for the pictures of Pam's vacation. On each line, write a word from the box.**

details	disappoint	forcibly
information	oceans	stroke

See the star I found? I didn't know stars

lived in **(1)** _____. I tried

to **(2)** _____ its back.

I wanted to take my star home, but Mom

stopped me **(3)** _____.

"I'm sorry to **(4)** _____ you,
but you have to stay here," I told the star.

"There are a lot of **(5)** _____
about stars in my book, but there isn't any

(6) _____ at all about stars
like you!"

TRY THIS!

There are many creatures that live in the ocean. Choose one
and write three sentences about it, using as many Vocabulary
Words as possible.

Name _____

Skill Reminder • **Some describing words tell how something tastes, smells, sounds, or feels.**

▶ Read the words under each line. Choose the describing word that tells how something tastes, smells, sounds, or feels. Write it on the line.

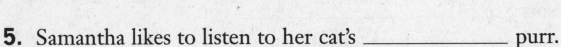

1. Samantha likes _____ snacks.

(saw   sweet   song)

2. Her cat likes _____ snacks.

(salty   say   seed)

3. Samantha eats _____ crackers.

(crunchy   cry   calm)

4. Her cat eats _____ cat food.

(door   dry   do)

5. Samantha likes to listen to her cat's _____ purr.

(loud   let's   lake)

6. She does not like her cat's _____ claws.

(sick   sharp   sorry)

7. Most of all, she likes her cat's _____ smell.

(sat   sweet   star)

8. Her cat likes to rub against the _____ rug.

(rough   read   roll)

Practice Book
Banner Days

Name _____

Syllable Rule • Divide a compound word between the two smaller words in it.

Examples: hot/dog   sail/boat

Dear Mr. Blueberry

Syllable Pattern: Compound Words

▶ Read the words in the box. Write each word in syllables.

heartache	backpack	sunshine	headband
floormat	blackboard	childcare	tonight
healthcare	highway	bookstore	football

Compound Words

1. _____ 5. _____ 9. _____

2. _____ 6. _____ 10. _____

3. _____ 7. _____ 11. _____

4. _____ 8. _____ 12. _____

▶ Write a sentence for three of the words.

13. _____

14. _____

15. _____

© Harcourt

Practice Book
Banner Days

Name _____

▶ **Read the paragraph. Then choose the best answer to each question. Fill in the circle next to your choice.**

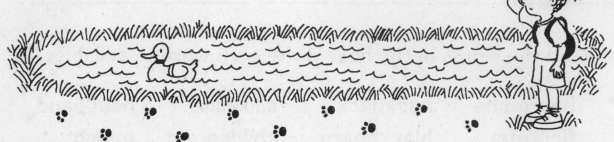

   Leisha walked to the pond to look for her dog, Tricks. There were wet dog tracks leading from the pond to the grass. Leisha followed the tracks. Then she heard a bark. It was Tricks! He was soaking wet. She quickly pulled a towel out of her backpack.

1. Most likely, Tricks was wet because

   ○ he played in the sprinklers.

   ○ it rained.

   ○ he ran under a water hose.

   ○ he swam in the pond.

> **Tip**
> Reread the paragraph to make sure you have the important information.

2. Which part of the paragraph helped you with the first question?

   ○ Leisha walked to the pond.

   ○ There were wet dog tracks leading from the pond.

   ○ Leisha followed the tracks.

   ○ She quickly pulled a towel out of her backpack.

> **Tip**
> Reread the first question. Which sentence might tell how the dog got wet?

SCHOOL-HOME CONNECTION Read a favorite story with your child. Help your child use story clues to make sentences about the characters and setting.

24

Practice Book
Banner Days

© Harcourt

▶ **Read the story. On each line, write the missing letters *gn*, *kn*, or *wr* that will complete each word.**

I **(1)** _____ew this day would be special. Dad cut the cake

with a **(2)** _____ife. I **(3)** _____ote a special card for Grandma.

Mom said I am a good **(4)** _____iter. We all **(5)** si_____ed it.

My brother **(6)** _____ocked on Grandma's door. The surprise

was **(7)** un_____own to Grandma. She smiled when she saw the

kitten curled around my **(8)** _____ist.

SCHOOL-HOME CONNECTION Invite your child to write three original sentences using words from this lesson.

25

Practice Book
Banner Days

▶ **Complete the picture labels. Write a word from the box on each line.**

| thief | wife | leaf | elf | shelf |
| thieves | wives | leaves | elves | shelves |

1. Three _____ dance.

   One _____ sings.

2. A _____ falls.

   Many _____ stay on the tree.

3. An _____ wakes up.

   Two _____ sleep.

4. Three _____ are full.

   One _____ is empty.

5. A _____ runs away.

   Two _____ stay.

SCHOOL-HOME CONNECTION Have your child write the words from the lesson. Ask your child to use a blue crayon to circle the f in each singular word and the v in each plural word. Talk about how each word changed.

26

► **Read the Spelling Words. Sort the words and write them where they belong.**

Spelling Words

Ends with *f* or *fe*	Ends with *ves*
1. _____	6. _____
2. _____	7. _____
3. _____	8. _____
4. _____	9. _____
5. _____	10. _____

wife
wives
leaf
leaves
elf
elves
shelf
shelves
life
lives
rooftop
true
bone
draw
whose

► **Write the words that are left in alphabetical order.**

11. _____	14. _____
12. _____	15. _____
13. _____	

Name _____

▶ **Circle and write the word that best completes each sentence.**

1. I will bring a _____ of bread to the picnic.

loaf   loafs   loaves

2. I think we need two _____ of bread.

loafs   loaves   loaf

3. Anne's paints and crayons are on the two bottom

_____ of the closet.

shelf   shelves   shelfs

4. Let's take the umbrella on the top _____ in case it rains.

shelf   shelfs   shelves

5. Did you invite Anne's art teacher and his _____ to the picnic?

wife   wifes   wives

6. Yes, I asked all of Anne's teachers and their _____ and husbands to come.

wifes   wives   wive

7. Did you see the picture she drew of the two _____ in the barn?

calf   calfs   calves

28

Practice Book
Banner Days

© Harcourt

Name _____

▶ **Complete the sentences. On each line, write a word from the paint jars.**

mimicked · fussed · pale · admired · notice · haze

Jake liked the **(1)** _____ colors in this painting.

"There's a blue **(2)** _____ over the hills," he said.

In another painting, baby birds **(3)** _____ for food.

Jake **(4)** _____ the mother bird. "Did you

(5) _____ how real that apple looks?" Jake asked. Can

you guess which painting Jake **(6)** _____ most of all?

TRY THIS! Write three sentences about a person you admire. Use as many Vocabulary Words as possible. Draw a picture to go with your sentences.

Name _____

Skill Reminder • Some describing words tell
how many.

▶ In each sentence, circle the describing word that tells how
many. Then think of another describing word that tells how
many. Write your new sentence.

1. Three boys row on the lake.

_____

2. Two grown-ups help them.

_____

3. They have three fishing poles.

_____

4. They want to catch seven fish.

_____

5. There are five other boats on the lake.

_____

6. Four girls swim in the lake.

_____

7. Ten children fish from the shore.

_____

8. Seven ducks swim by.

_____

© Harcourt

Practice Book
Banner Days

Syllable Rule • Divide a compound word between the two smaller words in it.

Examples: hot/dog   sail/boat

▶ **Read the words in the box. Write each word in syllables. Use slash marks to separate the syllables.**

birthday	broadcast	catfish	sidewalk
daydream	cowboy	sunshine	horseshoe
rainbow	pinpoint	moonlight	bookstore

Compound Words

1. _____

2. _____

3. _____

4. _____

5. _____

6. _____

7. _____

8. _____

9. _____

10. _____

11. _____

12. _____

Name _____

▶ **Read the paragraph. Then choose the best answer to each question. Fill in the circle next to your choice.**

Judy liked to paint. She painted pictures of her family on paper. She painted a picture of a <u>happy</u> frog with a smile on his face. She painted a <u>light</u> blue star on a dark blue chair. Then she tried to paint a beard on her father. That's when her parents took her paints away. Now Judy uses crayons.

1. An antonym for *happy* is—

○ joyful

○ glad

○ sad

○ merry

 Tip
Look for a word with the opposite meaning.

2. An antonym for *light* is—

○ dark

○ clear

○ white

○ bright

 Tip
Be sure to fill in the circle completely.

SCHOOL-HOME CONNECTION With your child, make a list of a few words and their antonyms. Discuss the differences between the meanings.

32

Practice Book
Banner Days

© Harcourt

Name _____

▶ **Read the story. On each line, write the abbreviation that stands for the underlined word.**

I have a very busy life. Every <u>Tuesday</u>
I ride my bike to Pine <u>Street</u>. I meet
<u>Missus</u> Walker for my piano lesson. I
practice hard for my recital in <u>August</u>.
On <u>Wednesday</u> I play soccer in the
park. My coach is <u>Mister</u> Reed. In
<u>December</u> and <u>January</u> I go skating
at the rink. Sometimes I like <u>Sunday</u>
best. That's when I sleep late.

1. _____

2. _____

3. _____

4. _____

5. _____

6. _____

7. _____

8. _____

9. _____

SCHOOL-HOME CONNECTION Have your child go on an abbreviation search and list any abbreviations he or she finds. Guide your child to check places like calendars, phone books, and appointment cards.

© Harcourt

Name _____

▶ **Finish the story. On each line, write a word from the box.**

standing	freezing	doing	slowly
swimming	eating	taking	actually

A Very Cool Dream

Last night I dreamed I visited Antarctica.

My family and I were **(1)** _____

staying in a hotel made of ice! "What will we be

(2) _____ first," I asked my dad. He said,

"We'll be **(3)** _____ our breakfast soon." My sister

wanted to go **(4)** _____ in the pool. Later, we were

(5) _____ in the **(6)** _____ wind. My

mom was **(7)** _____ pictures of us. Then I

(8) _____ began to wake up. I was so cold! My

blanket had fallen off the bed!

SCHOOL-HOME CONNECTION With your child, write a funny story about a vacation. Have your child use words with -ing and -ly endings.

34

Practice Book
Banner Days

© Harcourt

Name _____

▶ **Read the Spelling Words. Sort the words and write them where they belong.**

Spelling Words

Words with *ing*	
1. _____	6. _____
2. _____	7. _____
3. _____	**Words with *ly***
4. _____	8. _____
5. _____	9. _____
	10. _____

completely
actually
doing
taking
swimming
eating
slowly
starting
standing
freezing
leaf
leaves
important
nothing
dinner

▶ **Sort the words that are left by the number of syllables.**

One-Syllable Words	Two-Syllable Word
11. _____	13. _____
12. _____	14. _____
	Three-Syllable Word
	15. _____

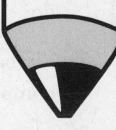

Practice Book
Banner Days

Name _____

▶ **Circle and write the word that best completes each sentence.**

1. I am _____ to deliver newspapers.
   start   stop   starting

2. I fold each newspaper _____.
   careful   carefully   care

3. I am _____ money to buy a book.
   earning   earned   earn

4. I like _____ my bike.
   ride   riding   rode

5. I ride _____ down the street.
   slowing   slowly   slow

6. I am _____ a good job.
   do   doing   did

7. My bag is _____ empty now.
   completely   complete   completing

8. I like _____ my book about penguins!
   read   reading   reads

SCHOOL-HOME CONNECTION Ask your child to list some ways that people earn money. Help your child to include words that end with *-ing*.

36

Practice Book
Banner Days

© Harcourt

▶ **Solve the riddles. On each line, write a word from the box.**

flippers	**hatch**	**horizon**
miserable	**slippery**	**waddled**

1. You walk on a wet floor and fall. Why?

   The floor is _____.

2. You are at the beach. The sun is going down. What do you

   see? The sun is setting over the _____.

3. Penguins do not have wings. What do they have?

   Penguins have _____.

4. You have a cold and can't go ice-skating with your friends.

   How do you feel? You feel _____.

5. A mother duck just laid three eggs. What will happen?

   The eggs will _____.

6. The ducklings walked toward
   their mother. How did they walk?

   The ducklings _____.

Name _____

Skill Reminder • **A describing word that ends with _er_ compares one thing with another thing. A describing word that ends with _est_ compares one thing with two or more other things.**

▶ **Add _er_ or _est_ to the describing word in ( ). Write the new word on the line.**

1. The air is _____ than the water. **(cold)**

2. This is the _____ place on Earth. **(cold)**

3. This wave is _____ than that wave. **(high)**

4. That is the _____ bird I have ever seen. **(big)**

5. The water is _____ over here than over there. **(deep)**

6. That bird's egg is _____ than this bird's egg. **(small)**

7. Summer is the _____ time of year. **(warm)**

8. We climbed the _____ hill of all. **(tall)**

TRY THIS! Draw a picture of three short animals that are different heights. Write a sentence about each animal. Use the words _short_, _shorter_, and _shortest_ in your sentences.

© Harcourt

Name _____

▶ **Choose the word in which *ing* or *ly* is added correctly. Fill in the circle next to your choice.**

Example: win
- ○ wining
- ○ winning
- ○ wineing

1 extreme
- ○ extremly
- ○ extremmly
- ○ extremely

Tip
Ignore the choice that is clearly wrong.

2 run
- ○ running
- ○ runeing
- ○ runing

Tip
Think about the rules before you choose.

3 trace
- ○ tracing
- ○ traceing
- ○ traccing

© Harcourt

▶ **Read the book titles and their descriptions.**
Then answer the questions. Write your
answers on the lines.

All About Eggs
by
Annie Dune

This book describes the eggs of many different birds. Photos are included.

Bird Watching
by
Emma Gordon

This book gives information about where to find different kinds of birds. It includes maps and diagrams.

Bird Tales
by
Jeff Greene

This book tells of a talking penguin and his adventures on the Arctic ice.

💡**Tip**
Nonfiction gives information.

1. Which books are nonfiction?

_____

_____

💡**Tip**
Fiction sometimes includes things that could not happen in real life.

2. Which book is fiction?

_____

_____

© Harcourt

▶ **Read the story. On each line, write the plural of the underlined word.**

Carla has many **(1)** hobby. She likes to garden. She calls the plants her **(2)** baby. In the park, she likes to look at the **(3)** poppy. She knows that gardeners have many **(4)** duty. It is not easy to grow **(5)** beauty like these. Carla also likes to learn about different **(6)** country. She goes to **(7)** library to get books about them. She collects coins and has the most **(8)** penny.

1. _____

2. _____

3. _____

4. _____

5. _____

6. _____

7. _____

8. _____

SCHOOL-HOME CONNECTION Ask your child to write three sentences with plurals. Then ask him or her to tell you the singular for each plural word he or she used.

41

Practice Book
Banner Days

Name _____

▶ **Finish the story. On each line, write a word from the box.**

remove	**return**	**recycle**	**replace**
recall	**preheat**	**preschool**	**preview**

A Trip to the Library

Mona wanted to **(1)** _____ her mystery book to the library. On the way, she dropped off newspapers

in the **(2)** _____ bin. She waved to the

(3) _____ children playing in the park. The

librarian asked Mona to **(4)** _____ her bookmark.

"I want to **(5)** _____ this mystery book with

another one," Mona said. "Would you like a

(6) _____ of our new books?" the librarian asked.

Mona couldn't **(7)** _____ when she'd had such

an enjoyable day! At home, she asked her mom to

(8) _____ the oven. She wanted to bake a cake for

the librarian!

SCHOOL-HOME CONNECTION Ask your child to choose four words from the box. Have your child write the words and circle the prefixes *pre-* or *re-* in each word. Ask your child to tell you what the words mean.

42

Practice Book
Banner Days

© Harcourt

▶ **Read the Spelling Words. Sort the words and write them where they belong.**

Words with *re*	Words with *pre*
1. _____	6. _____
2. _____	7. _____
3. _____	8. _____
4. _____	9. _____
5. _____	10. _____

Spelling Words

remove
return
recycle
replace
recall
preheat
prepay
preschool
preview
prefix
swimming
doing
maybe
near
park

▶ **Sort the words that are left by the number of syllables.**

One-Syllable Words	Two-Syllable Words
11. _____	13. _____
12. _____	14. _____
	15. _____

43

► **Finish the sentences. Write a word from the box on each line.**

| reread | prefix | remove | refill | recycle | preschool |

1. Very young children go to this school.

   It's a _____.

2. You do this when you are finished with

   newspapers and glass jars. You _____.

3. This is a word part at the beginning of a word. It's a

   _____.

4. You do this to your muddy boots before you go inside.

   You _____ them.

5. You do this when you like a book so much you want to read

   it again.

   You _____ it.

6. You do this to your glass when you want

   more to drink. You _____ it.

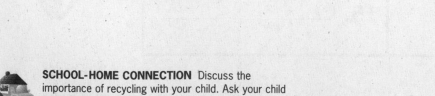

SCHOOL-HOME CONNECTION Discuss the
importance of recycling with your child. Ask your child
to think of other words with the prefix *re-*. Discuss
how the prefix changes the meaning of the word to
mean *again*.

44

Practice Book
Banner Days

© Harcourt

▶ **Finish the story. On each line, write a word from the box.**

caused	clasp	confused	cornered
objects	removes	typical	

1. Annie almost never

_____ her watch.
One day she left the

_____ open. This

_____ her watch
to fall off.

2. Her cat, Sammy, always

spots _____ on
the floor. "This isn't just a

_____ cat toy,"
Sammy thought.

3. He picked up the watch.
Then it started to beep!
Sammy was

_____.

4. "Sammy!" Annie said. "You
have my watch

_____!"

© Harcourt

45

Skill Reminder • **An action verb tells what someone or something does. A verb can tell about an action that is happening now.**

▶ **Read the sentences. Then read the words under each line. Choose the word that is a verb. Write it on the line.**

1. I _____ on the bench.
   (so sit stove)

2. You _____ past the bench.
   (walk well way)

3. I _____ hello to you.
   (say she sea)

4. You _____ around.
   (to turn tale)

5. We _____ for a while.
   (talk two table)

6. Then we _____ to the swings.
   (good go green)

7. We _____ there.
   (pill play pond)

8. We _____ home together.
   (walk white whale)

© Harcourt

Syllable Rule • **Divide a word between the prefix and the base word.**
Examples: re/read   un/kind

▶ **Add a prefix to the base word to create a new word that makes sense in the sentence. Write the new word on the line, dividing it into syllables.**

1. We plan to _____ the new movie.

view

pre-   un-

2. I hope to _____ my old hometown.

visit

re-   un-

3. Ben was _____ to stay up so late.

wise

un-   pre-

4. She _____ her napkin to eat dinner.

fold

pre-   un-

5. We will _____ home after dark.

turn

un-   re-

Practice Book
Banner Days

Name _____

▶ **Read the story. Then choose the best answer to each question. Fill in the circle next to your choice.**

The Mystery of the Missing Baseball Glove

John could not find his baseball glove. His game was in an hour. He ran all around the house looking for the glove. He looked under his bed. He looked under the table. Finally, he looked under his cat, Smoke. Smoke was sleeping on the glove!

1. What is the problem in this story's plot? ——

○ John likes to play baseball.

○ John has a cat named Smoke.

○ John has a baseball game.

○ John lost his baseball glove.

> **Tip**
> Reread the story to help you find the answer.

2. How is the problem solved? ——

○ John finds the glove under his bed.

○ John finds the glove under the table.

○ John finds the glove under the cat.

○ John finds the glove in his backpack.

> **Tip**
> Carefully read each answer choice.

© Harcourt

SCHOOL-HOME CONNECTION With your child, make up a story about someone who has lost something. Ask your child to tell you the story's main problem and how it is solved.

48

Practice Book
Banner Days

Name _____

▶ **Write the word from the box that best
completes each sentence in the story.**

misplaced	underline	underdog	underfed

A Doggy Tale

Nancy **(1)** _____ her favorite pen. She used the pen

to **(2)** _____ words she liked. Instead of finding her

pen, Nancy found a hungry, and **(3)** _____ puppy.
Nancy took the puppy home and fed it. The dog got strong and
frisky. "You were unlucky, " Nancy said to her puppy. "Now you
have a family that loves you. You are an

(4) _____ that won!"

SCHOOL-HOME CONNECTION With your child,
make a list of words that begin with *mis-* or *under-*.
Circle the base word in each word. Ask your child to
choose three words, and write two sentences for
each word, using the base word in one sentence and
the word with a prefix in the second sentence.

49

© Harcourt

Name _____

▶ **Circle the best answer to each riddle.**

1. You have one above
each eye.   **bring   brow   bray**

2. A circle is this shape.   **round   rained   road**

3. This is something
you hear.   **sound   send   sand**

4. Rain falls from this.   **could   cloud   called**

5. People live in this.   **hands   horse   house**

6. This is used to
make bread.   **flare   flyer   flour**

7. You use this to speak.   **math   mouth   moth**

8. This is a kind of bird.   **oil   owl   only**

9. This tells how
something could sound.   **land   laid   loud**

10. It is a small animal.   **mouse   moist   moose**

© Harcourt

SCHOOL-HOME CONNECTION With your child, make up a story about a mouse that lives in your house. Use as many words with the *ou* sound as you can.

50

Practice Book
Banner Days

▶ **Finish the story. On each line, write a word from the box.**

I'll	can't	don't	they'll
we'll	you'll	shouldn't	that's

Packing for Camp

"Tim, have you finished packing? **(1)** _____

be here soon," Dad said. "**(2)** _____ be finished

in a minute," Tim answered. "I **(3)** _____ wait

to go. I just **(4)** _____ know if I should pack

my boots," he said. "Since **(5)** _____ probably

ride horses there, you **(6)** _____ forget your

boots," Mom said. "But I think you should wear them instead

of packing them." At last, Tim finished. "Well, I guess

(7) _____ it!"
he said. "And just in time, too!
The van is here!" Dad said.
"Have fun!" his parents called.

"**(8)** _____ write you lots of letters!"

SCHOOL-HOME CONNECTION With your child, discuss what you pack when you go on a trip. Ask your child to use three contractions from the word box in sentences that tell about packing.

51

Practice Book
Banner Days

▶ **Read the Spelling Words. Write the contractions in alphabetical order.**

Contractions	
1. _____	6. _____
2. _____	7. _____
3. _____	8. _____
4. _____	9. _____
5. _____	10. _____

▶ **Write the words that are left in alphabetical order.**

11. _____	14. _____
12. _____	15. _____
13. _____	

Spelling Words

we'll
I'll
you'll
they'll
don't
can't
isn't
it's
that's
shouldn't
preheat
recycle
shop
surprise
kittens

© Harcourt

Name _____

► **Circle and write the word that best completes each sentence.**

1. _____ give my teacher a party.

   Well   **We'll**   **We'will**

2. It _____ a good-bye party.

   isn't   **isnt**   **is'not**

3. _____ a "We Like You" party!

   It'is   **Its**   **It's**

4. _____ the best kind!

   That's   **That'is**   **Thats**

5. We _____ wait!

   cann't   **can'not**   **can't**

6. _____ get a cake.

   She'll   **She'will**   **Shell**

7. We _____ make noise.

   shouldn't   **shouldno't**   **should't**

8. _____ surprised!

   Shes   **She's**   **She'is**

© Harcourt

53

Practice Book
Banner Days

Name _____

▶ **Complete the sentences. On each line, write a word from the box.**

addresses	clerk	grown	honor	pour	route

We Love You, Mrs. King!

We are having a party in _____ of Mrs. King.

She drives the bus on our _____.

My brother is _____ up
now, but he used to ride Mrs. King's bus, too.

She must know the _____ of
hundreds of students!

I'll go to the store to ask the _____ to
order us a cake.

I'll _____ cold drinks for everybody.

TRY THIS! Write sentences about a job you would like to have when you grow up. Use the Vocabulary Words in your sentences.

© Harcourt

Practice Book
Banner Days

54

Skill Reminder • **When the naming part of a sentence tells about one, add the letter *s* to most verbs. Do not add an *s* to the verb when the naming part tells about *I*, *you*, or more than one.**

▶ **Look at the verb in ( ). Decide if it needs an *s* to finish the sentence correctly. Write the verb on the line.**

1. The mail carrier _____ down the street. **(walk)**

2. He _____ a package for two children. **(bring)**

3. Jan and Jesse _____ to get the package. **(want)**

4. At last the package _____. **(come)**

5. The children _____ the package. **(open)**

6. Jan _____ a box of cookies. **(get)**

7. Jesse and Jan _____ all the presents. **(like)**

8. Jesse _____ a thank-you letter. **(write)**

 TRY THIS! Write a thank-you letter to someone who helps people. Tell that person why you like what he or she does.

Name _____

▶ **Choose the word that is the correct contraction for the words. Fill in the circle next to your choice.**

Example I am

○ Iam

○ I'm

○ Im

1 he is

○ hes

○ hee's

○ he's

2 let us

○ lets

○ let's

○ letts

> 💡**Tip**
> Remember that you are taking out letters, not adding them.

3 we will

○ we'll

○ wel'l

○ w'ell

> 💡**Tip**
> Remember that the apostrophe (') is placed where a letter was taken out.

© Harcourt

► **Read the paragraph. Then answer the
questions.**

Today there are two ways to write and send a letter. The old way
is to write a letter on paper. The new way is to write e-mail on a
computer. To send a paper letter, you put it in an envelope with an
address and a stamp. The post office takes your letter to the address.
To send e-mail, you press "send" and your e-mail goes to the other
person's computer. For a paper letter, you have to buy a stamp. It
does not cost anything to send e-mail. Both kinds of letters are ways
to send a message to another person.

Name two ways e-mail and a letter
written on paper are alike.

Tip
Look for the word "both"
in the paragraph.

1. _____

2. _____

Tip
Reread the paragraph
for details you may
have missed.

3. Paper letters go through _____, but

e-mail goes from your computer _____

4. You have to buy _____ to send _____,

but e-mail is _____.

SCHOOL-HOME CONNECTION Gather some
of your child's favorite toys. Ask your child to
compare and contrast the toys.

57

Practice Book
Banner Days

© Harcourt

Name _____

▶ **Read the story. On each line, write the form of the underlined word that makes the sentence correct.**

I have two **(1)** <u>shelf</u> on my wall filled with books. I like to read tales about the woods. Every fall I walk in the woods to find **(2)** <u>leaf</u>. I read about five **(3)** <u>elf</u> who live in the woods. One small **(4)** <u>elves</u> wore a **(5)** <u>leaves</u> for a hat. If I could find that hat, I would build a special **(6)** <u>shelves</u> for it! I would ask the elf what his **(7)** <u>lives</u> is like. Maybe he would tell me about the **(8)** <u>life</u> of all the elves!

1. _____

2. _____

3. _____

4. _____

5. _____

6. _____

7. _____

8. _____

Practice Book
Banner Days

© Harcourt

► **Complete the sentences. On each line, write a word with the same vowel sound as *chew*.**

1. That shiny car must be _____.
(seen   new   near)

2. We made a thick vegetable _____.
(sandwich   snack   stew)

3. Orange _____ is good for you.
(juice   candy   day)

4. The _____ on the tree is ripe.
(fruit   leaves   light)

5. The pitcher _____ the ball fast.
(threw   ran   hit)

© Harcourt

SCHOOL-HOME CONNECTION Ask your child to draw and label pictures of a suit and a screw. Have your child underline the letters that make the vowel sound in each word.

Practice Book
Banner Days

▶ **Read the Spelling Words. Sort the words and write them where they belong.**

Words with *ew*	Words with *ui*
1. _____	6. _____
2. _____	7. _____
3. _____	8. _____
4. _____	9. _____
5. _____	10. _____

▶ **Sort the words that are left by the number of syllables.**

One-Syllable Words	Two-Syllable Words
11. _____	13. _____
12. _____	14. _____
	15. _____

Spelling Words

new
crew
stew
grew
threw
bruise
fruit
pursuit
juice
recruit
you'll
shouldn't
church
windows
sisters

© Harcourt

60

Name _____

▶ **Solve the riddles. Write a word from the box
on each line.**

new	juice	screw	grew	chew
crew	pursuit	threw	stew	flew

1. If a pitcher pitched a ball, he did

   this. He _____ it.

2. If a drum was just bought, it is this. It is _____.

3. When a plant got taller, it did this. It _____.

4. This can be a drink made from fruit. It is _____.

5. A thick soup is called this. It is _____.

6. This means chasing someone. You are in _____.

7. We do this when we eat. We _____.

8. We use this to make a repair. It's a _____.

9. These are the people who work on a boat.

   They're a _____.

10. When a bird went away, it did this. It _____.

© Harcourt

SCHOOL-HOME CONNECTION Ask your child to
divide the words into two groups. Have your child list
words spelled with *ew* in one group and words
spelled with *ui* in the other group.

61

Practice Book
Banner Days

Name _____

▶ **Finish the story. On each line, write a word from the drums.**

appeared

imitated

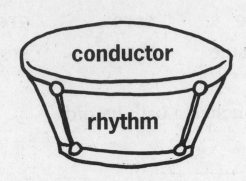

conductor

rhythm

created

startled

Jen asked Mr. Strong, the train **(1)** _____, for

an old box. She **(2)** _____ a drum by putting a lid on

the box. Slowly she began to beat out a **(3)** _____.

Boom boom–boom BOOM! The noise **(4)** _____ two

girls who were walking by. "I like that sound. Let's dance!" one of

them said.

Then a man and a woman **(5)** _____. They

both **(6)** _____ the steps the girls were doing. Soon all

the people on the street were tapping their feet!

 TRY THIS! Write a few sentences about the music you enjoy most. Use
at least three Vocabulary Words.

Practice Book
Banner Days

Name _____

Skill Reminder	• **A verb can tell about action in**

the past. Add *ed* to most verbs to tell about the past.

▶ **Look at the word in ( ). On the line, write the word to tell about the past.**

1. Yesterday Lee _____ up to the door. **(walk)**

2. She _____ the doorbell. **(push)**

3. My big brother _____ the door. **(open)**

4. Lee _____ for me. **(ask)**

5. I _____ Lee with a big smile. **(greet)**

6. I _____ toward my room. **(point)**

7. Lee _____ by me to look. **(rush)**

8. She _____ to see my new drum set. **(want)**

 TRY THIS! Write four sentences about something you did last week. In your sentences, use verbs that end with *ed*.

Syllable Rule In a word with the VC/V pattern, divide after the consonant when the first vowel is short. Example: lem/on

▶ Read the words in the box. Then write each word, dividing it into syllables.

| civil | habit | model | shovel | study |

fin/ish

1. _____

2. _____

3. _____

4. _____

5. _____

Name _____

Max Found Two
Sticks

**Multiple-Meaning
Words**
TEST PREP

▶ **Choose the meaning the underlined word has
in the sentence.**

1. The school band got to the
park early.

- ○ to stop a car in a place
- ○ an open place where
  people can play

> 💡 **Tip**
> Notice that *park* can be an
> action word and a naming
> word. In which way is the
> word used in the sentence?

2. The air was still chilly.

- ○ quiet
- ○ up to this time

> 💡 **Tip**
> Which meaning makes more
> sense?

3. She drummed a fast beat.

- ○ a regular rhythm
- ○ to win instead of
  someone else

> 💡 **Tip**
> Think about what a
> drummer does when he or
> she is playing.

SCHOOL-HOME CONNECTION With your child,
make a list of words that have more than one
meaning. Make up sentences with the different
meanings.

65

Practice Book
Banner Days

© Harcourt

▶ **Write the words from the box that best
complete the poem. Remember that the word
you write should rhyme with the underlined
word in the line above.**

voice	joy	toy	noise

Across the street there lived a ___boy___

Who played and played with just one _____,

A tiny whale the boy called ___Roy___.

All day long Roy gave him _____.

They'd run and jump with other ___boys___

And always make a lot of _____.

Alone at night if the boy had a ___choice___

He would talk to his toy in a quiet _____.

SCHOOL-HOME CONNECTION Discuss your
child's favorite toys and games. With your child, write
a short poem about a favorite toy. Remind your child
to use at least two words with the oi sound.

66

© Harcourt

▶ **Finish the story. On each line, write a word from the box.**

petroglyphs	**photo**	**telephone**	**paragraph**
laugh	**rough**	**cough**	**tough**

Finding a Treasure

Alda climbed over the **(1)** _____ rocks.

It was **(2)** _____
getting up the mountain. Finally, she was
at the top. She was so happy she started to

(3) _____. At the top

she saw some rocks with **(4)** _____. Then

she took a **(5)** _____ of the carvings.
She ran down the mountain so fast that she started to

(6) _____. When she got home, she

called the book store on the **(7)** _____.
She bought a book on treasures. There was a

(8) _____ on petroglyphs and a picture
of the rock Alda had found.

SCHOOL-HOME CONNECTION With your child talk
about things that make him or her laugh. Encourage
your child to write sentences describing these things,
using as many *ph* or *gh* words as possible.

67

Practice Book
Banner Days

Name _____

▶ **Read the Spelling Words. Sort the words
and write them where they belong.**

Words with *gh*	Words with *ph*
1. _____	6. _____
2. _____	7. _____
3. _____	8. _____
4. _____	9. _____
5. _____	10. _____

Spelling Words

paragraph
petroglyphs
photo
telephone
graph
laugh
cough
rough
enough
tough
pursuit
recruit
birthday
buy
dance

▶ **Sort the words that are left by the number
of syllables.**

One-Syllable Words	Two-Syllable Words
11. _____	13. _____
12. _____	14. _____
	15. _____

Practice Book
Banner Days

Name _____

▶ **Circle and write the word that best completes the sentence.**

1. Roberto had a _____ and stayed home.
cough   camp   corn

2. He still had a _____ to write for homework.
paragraph   party   petrograph

3. He thought, "I have done _____ for today."
every   enough   earning

4. Roberto closed this book on _____ .
funny   phony   phonics

5. He did not finish his _____ for math class.
graph   great   grass

6. It was a _____ choice to make.
touch   tough   teach

7. He called his friend Pedro on the _____ .
telegraph   television   telephone

8. "May I borrow your book of funny _____ ?"
Roberto asked.
forever   phonetic   photographs

SCHOOL-HOME CONNECTION With your child make a list
of words that begin with the letters *ph*. Choose two words and
write a sentence for each word. Then have your
child draw a picture that tells about the sentence.

69

Practice Book
Banner Days

© Harcourt

Name _____

▶ **Finish the ad. On each line, write a word from the box.**

| dappled exhibition landscape business ranch thousands |

**Come and stay
for a week
or two at
Misty Meadow!**

MISTY MEADOW

You will love
your vacation at our

beautiful _____. Ride a _____ horse

across the hills. Make a lasso and take part in a roping

_____. Walk in our new flower garden, cared for

by our own _____.

At Misty Meadow, you will feel you are _____

of miles from the city!

© Harcourt

TRY THIS! Draw a picture of a place where you would like to go on vacation. Write two or three sentences about your picture. Use as many Vocabulary Words as you can.

Practice Book
Banner Days

Name _____

Skill Reminder • Some verbs tell what someone or something is like.

• *Am*, *is*, and *are* tell about now. *Was* and *were* tell about the past.

▶ These sentences tell about now. Write *am*, *is*, or *are* to complete each sentence.

1. This rope _____ big.

2. It _____ a gift for me.

3. I _____ very happy!

4. My horses _____ happy, too.

▶ These sentences tell about the past. Write *was* or *were* to complete each sentence.

5. Mr. Fox _____ my teacher.

6. Tasha and Sophie _____ in the class, too.

7. We _____ good riders.

8. I _____ the best!

 TRY THIS! Work with a partner. Take turns telling about yourselves. Use the verbs *am*, *is*, *are*, *was*, and *were*.

Practice Book
Banner Days

Name _____

▶ **Choose the word that has the same sound as the underlined letters in the first word. Fill in the circle next to your choice.**

Example ne<u>ph</u>ew

     ○ niece

     ○ five

     ○ review

1 lau<u>gh</u>

     ○ lazy

     ○ phrase

     ○ gravy

💡 Tip

Be sure you know the sound the underlined letters make. If you are not sure about the sounds in one word, look down the page and find other words that you might know that have a **gh** or **ph**.

2 tele<u>ph</u>one

     ○ television

     ○ bone

     ○ enough

💡 Tip

Say the first word aloud and listen to the sound the underlined letters make. Then read each answer choice and listen for the same sound.

3 lau<u>gh</u>ing

     ○ elephant

     ○ lacking

     ○ going

© Harcourt

Practice Book
Banner Days

▶ **Read the story. Then answer the questions.**

Kit and Sunny

Kit had a horse named Sunny. Sunny was a beautiful black horse. It had a white star on its forehead. One day, Kit took Sunny out for a ride. When Kit rode past the town bank, she saw the robber, No Good Ned. Sunny and Kit chased the robber. He was running out with a sack of gold. Kit used her lasso to catch No Good Ned. Sunny and Kit saved the day!

1. Which sentence is important enough to put in a summary of this story?

Kit and Sunny caught a robber. *Or*

Kit's horse was black with a white star.

_____

_____

Tip

Remember that a summary tells what a story is mostly about.

2. Which sentence is **not** important enough to put in a summary of this story?

Kit used her lasso to catch the robber. *Or*

Sunny was a great horse.

_____

_____

Tip

A summary tells only the most important events.

© Harcourt

SCHOOL-HOME CONNECTION Read a short story or newspaper article to your child. Ask your child to summarize and retell the story.

Practice Book
Banner Days

▶ **Circle the best answer to each riddle.**

1. The sky is this color. **boil   blue   bell**

2. This can stick things together. **goal   girl   glue**

3. Twelve o'clock is this time. **nine   moon   noontime**

4. You can visit animals there. **zoo   zip   zap**

5. You use this to sweep. **broom   bring   broil**

6. You use this to eat soup. **spoil   spoon   space**

7. These men ride horses. **cook   cowboy   cool**

8. If something is not false it is this. **true   tree   tray**

9. A kitchen is one of these. **roof   room   roast**

10. We use these to speak. **vases   voices   votes**

© Harcourt

SCHOOL-HOME CONNECTION Play *I Went to the Zoo* with your child. Start by saying, "I went to the zoo and I took my boot." Have your child repeat the sentence and add another word with the *oo* sound. Continue by taking turns naming appropriate items.

74

Practice Book
Banner Days

Name _____

▶ **Finish the story. On each line, write a word from the box.**

smarter	tallest	smallest	fresher
smartest	taller	freshest	

Grandma's building is **(1)** _____ than my house.

She lives in a city with some of the **(2)** _____ buildings in the world. The food on our farm is

(3) _____ than the food in the grocery store in the city. We grow our food in the garden. When my grandma visits

us, she says, "Han, you have the **(4)** _____ food I

have ever eaten." Even though she has the **(5)** _____ hands in our family, she can do almost anything. "You are the

(6) _____ person I have ever met," I tell her. She gives me a hug and says, "When you grow up, you will be

(7) _____ than I am."

SCHOOL-HOME CONNECTION Talk with your child about what life was like when you were in second grade. With your child, write sentences comparing how things were then with the way they are now. Encourage your child to use words with −er and −est endings.

75

© Harcourt

▶ **Read the Spelling Words. Sort the words and write them where they belong.**

Spelling Words

Words with *er*	Words with *est*
1. _____	6. _____
2. _____	7. _____
3. _____	8. _____
4. _____	9. _____
5. _____	10. _____

taller
tallest
fresher
freshest
smaller
smallest
smarter
smartest
happier
happiest
paragraph
telephone
lion
oil
men

▶ **Sort the words that are left by the number of syllables.**

One-Syllable Words	Three-Syllable Words
11. _____	14. _____
12. _____	15. _____
Two-Syllable Words	
13. _____	

© Harcourt

Name _____

▶ **Circle and write the word that best completes the sentence.**

1. Chinese New Year is the _____ day of the
year for my family. **happy   happier   happiest**

2. On that day my grandmother looks _____
than anyone.   **happy   happier   happiest**

3. We eat a _____ lunch than we usually do.
big   bigger   biggest

4. My grandmother cooks the _____ crabs she
can find.   **fresh   fresher   freshest**

5. My brother, Wen, tells the _____ stories he
knows.   **funny   funnier   funniest**

6. Then we make banners _____ than two
yardsticks.   **long   longer   longest**

7. At night we have the _____ parade I've
ever seen.   **large   larger   largest**

8. We dress up in the _____ costumes.
bright   brighter   brightest

9. My uncle wears a dragon mask with a

_____ mouth than his own.

wide   wider   widest

SCHOOL-HOME CONNECTION Talk about a
custom or holiday that you and your child enjoy. Ask
your child to write sentences describing what he or
she likes. Have your child use comparing words that
end in −er and −est.

77

Practice Book
Banner Days

© Harcourt

▶ **Complete the sentences. On each line, write a word from the box.**

| celebrations | develop | furious |
| graceful | grocery store | students |

1. Mom wanted me to get two cakes from the

   _____.

2. We were having parties for two

   _____ in my school.

3. I was _____

   when one cake fell on my way home!

4. I had to get another cake so the

   _____ could go on.

5. We worked hard to _____

   a list of games we could play.

6. At the parties, some of us did

   _____ cartwheels.

 TRY THIS! Draw a picture of yourself with a friend at a birthday party. Write about your picture. Use as many Vocabulary Words from the box as you can.

© Harcourt

Skill Reminder • *Has* and *have* tell about now.
Had tells about the past.

▶ **Complete the sentences. Write *has*, *have*, or *had*
on each line.**

1. Tasha _____ a great class last week.

2. Today she _____ new things to learn.

3. Her brothers _____ classes now, too.

4. Last week, they _____ a long class.

5. Now they _____ a shorter class.

6. Today the teacher

   _____ a show after class.

7. The students _____ fun
   watching the show.

8. Tasha _____ even
   more fun in class.

TRY THIS! Draw a picture of something that happened yesterday. Write about the picture, using the verb *had*. Then write about the picture as if it is happening now. Use the verbs that tell about now.

Name _____

Syllable Rule	**When a single consonant is**

between two vowels, divide before the consonant.
Try the first syllable long. If the word makes sense, keep it!
Example: ti/ger   pa/per

▶ Circle the V/CV word that solves each riddle.

1. When you don't work, you are this.
telegraph   sleeply   lazy   helpful

2. A small restaurant is called this.
diner   café   store   more

3. You use a camera to take one.
pots   floppy   photo   fitting

4. You use this to measure.
yardstick   graph   ruler   grease

5. This is a type of bird.
chicken   hawk   raven   robin

6. This is a day of the week.
Sunday   Tuesday   Friday   Monday

7. You do this to a door.
clog   open   close   keep

8. This is someone who rides.
jockey   walker   rider   route

© Harcourt

▶ **Read the paragraph and answer the questions.**

Chinese restaurants are popular all over the
United States. People like the many choices. You can get chicken,
beef, pork, or seafood mixed with all kinds of vegetables. You
can get vegetables and rice with no meat. You can get different
sauces. Another thing people like about Chinese restaurants is
the fast service. Most Chinese meals are cooked in a deep pan
with rounded sides. The pan, called a wok, cooks food quickly
and evenly.

1. Which sentence is an important
detail that supports the main
idea of the paragraph?

   ○ You can get a meal with
      no meat at all.

   ○ You can get different sauces.

   ○ People like the many choices.

> **Tip**
>
> Find the main idea.
> Then think about the
> important details that
> support the main idea.

2. Which sentence is an important
detail that supports the main
idea of the paragraph?

   ○ Another thing people like
      about Chinese restaurants
      is the fast service.

   ○ Meals are cooked in a deep
      pan with rounded sides.

   ○ The pan, called a wok, cooks food quickly and evenly.

> **Tip**
>
> Look for the more
> general statements.

SCHOOL-HOME CONNECTION With your child,
tell the story of an adventure you shared. Decide
which details support the main idea.

81

Practice Book
Banner Days

▶ **Circle the best answer to each riddle.**

1. This means very pretty.
   beautiful   bike   became   bake

2. This means full of thanks.
   think   thankful   thing   thin

3. A person who does not do things
   with care is this.
   carry   careless   crack   course

4. This means not good for you.
   handle   hold   harmful   himself

5. A person who does kind things is this.
   thank   through   thoughtful   three

6. Something that is not dangerous is this.
   healthy   hearth   harm   harmless

7. A person who has no fear is this.
   frightened   frown   fearless   funny

8. A person who is happy is this.
   cheerful   charm   check   careful

© Harcourt

SCHOOL-HOME CONNECTION Discuss the
meanings of these words with your child. Have your
child write five sentences using as many –ful and
–less words as possible.

82

Name _____

▶ **Write the words where they belong in the chart.**

| airport | airplanes | chair | careful | dare | share |
| rare | scare | hair | pair | stairs | stare |

air   **mare**

_____   _____

_____   _____

_____   _____

_____   _____

_____   _____

SCHOOL-HOME CONNECTION With your child make a list of *air* and *are* words. Ask your child to choose two words and write a sentence for each. Then have your child draw a picture to illustrate each sentence.

83

Practice Book
Banner Days

▶ **Read the Spelling Words. Sort the words and write them where they belong.**

Words with *air*	Words with *are*
1. _____	6. _____
2. _____	7. _____
3. _____	8. _____
4. _____	9. _____
5. _____	10. _____

Spelling Words

airport
airplanes
chair
careful
dare
share
rare
scare
hair
pair
tallest
happier
boat
city
morning

▶ **Write the words that are left in alphabetical order.**

11. _____	14. _____
12. _____	15. _____
13. _____	

© Harcourt

▶ **Circle and write the word that completes each sentence.**

1. In the morning Claire brushes her _____.

hair   half   harm

2. Today, her family is going on an _____.

airplane   armor   artist

3. They are going to the _____.

action   airport   actor

4. Claire _____ a sandwich with her brother.

shark   shorts   shares

5. She sits down on a _____.

choose   chair   chat

6. The plane will soar through the _____.

are   oar   air

7. She flaps her arms like a _____ of wings.

part   port   pair

8. "It would not _____ me to fly over the clouds," she says.

scare   scar   score

© Harcourt

SCHOOL-HOME CONNECTION Ask your child what it would be like to fly through the air. Encourage your child to write a sentence about how it would feel and what he or she might see. Have your child use words with *are* and *air*.

85

Practice Book
Banner Days

Name _____

▶ **Finish the ad. On each line, write a word from the box.**

| flock | glide | harbor | soared | swooping |

Take a ride in one of Red's Ready Planes!

Have you ever **(1)** _____ across the sky? Have you ever seen a

(2) _____ of birds flying and wished you could fly, too? You can do it in one of Red's Ready Planes! You will

(3) _____ over the city. You will sail above the boats in the

(4) _____. Call Red today.

Soon you will be **(5)** _____ through the sky!

TRY THIS! Imagine that you are a bird flying high in the sky. Write about what you see. Use as many Vocabulary Words as you can in your sentences.

Name _____

Skill Reminder • The verbs *see* and *give* tell about now. To tell what *he, she,* or *it* does, add *s*.
• The verbs *saw* and *gave* tell about the past.

▶ Read the words under each line.
Write the correct form of the
verb to finish the sentence.

1. Years ago, Ms. Torres _____ a bus
that she liked.   **(see saw)**

2. She _____ a man money and bought it.
(gave gives)

3. Now she _____ the bus every day.
(see sees)

4. Other people _____ the bus, too.
(see sees)

5. The people _____ Ms. Torres some money.
(gives give)

6. She _____ them a ride on the bus.
(gives give)

7. Last week, the people on the bus _____ a parade.
(sees saw)

8. The parade _____ everyone a thrill.
(give gave)

▶ **Choose the word that has the same sound as the underlined letters in the first word.**

Example: h<u>ai</u>r

    ○ heart

    ○ dare

    ○ rear

1 c<u>ar</u>e

    ○ car

    ○ ear

    ○ stair

> **Tip**
> Say each choice aloud. Be sure each word makes sense when you say it.

2 <u>ai</u>rport

    ○ artist

    ○ part

    ○ shared

> **Tip**
> Listen to the sound as you say each choice to yourself.

3 squ<u>are</u>

    ○ fairground

    ○ school

    ○ quiet

> **Tip**
> Be sure to fill in the circle completely.

▶ **Read the paragraph and answer the questions.**

Two men talked loudly. One man pointed at his watch and then looked at the door. He shook his head. Just then a third man walked through the door. The two men stopped talking and walked over to him. They pointed at their watches.

1. What do you think the two men are talking about?

_____

2. How do you know this?

_____

3. Is the third man late or on time?

_____

4. How do you know this?

_____

SCHOOL-HOME CONNECTION With your child, discuss common occurrences at home, such as making dinner and getting ready for school. Ask what signals help your child infer what is going on.

89

Practice Book
Banner Days

▶ **Read the story. Write each underlined word in the correct column on the chart.**

I am <u>going</u> to the park. There is a <u>swimming</u> pool in the park. It is <u>actually</u> a lot of fun. Sometimes, the water is <u>freezing</u>. Then I wade into the pool very <u>slowly</u>. <u>Lately</u>, it has been very hot during the day. So I jump right in off the <u>diving</u> board. I am <u>really</u> a very good swimmer.

-ing	**-ly**
1. _____	5. _____
2. _____	6. _____
3. _____	7. _____
4. _____	8. _____

Practice Book
Banner Days

© Harcourt

► **Write the words from the box where they belong in the chart. The words with *oo* go under *book*. The words with *ou* go under *would*.**

| look | could | hook | cook | boyhood |
| foot | childhood | stood | should | brook |

Book	**Would**
_____	_____
_____	_____
_____	
_____	
_____	
_____	
_____	

SCHOOL-HOME CONNECTION Ask your child to think of three things he or she would like to do. Then have your child write sentences about them, using the word *would*.

91

Practice Book
Banner Days

Name _____

▶ **Read the Spelling Words. Sort the words and write them where they belong.**

Spelling Words

Words with *oo*	6. _____
	7. _____
1. _____	**Words with *ou***
2. _____	
3. _____	8. _____
4. _____	9. _____
5. _____	10. _____

look
could
would
cook
book
boyhood
foot
childhood
stood
should
careful
chair
mountain
state
America

▶ **Sort the words that are left by the number of syllables.**

One-Syllable Words	Two-Syllable Words
11. _____	13. _____
12. _____	14. _____
	Four-Syllable word
	15. _____

© Harcourt

Name _____

▶ **Circle the word that best completes each sentence. Then write the word on the line.**

1. At camp we _____ over an open fire.
cold   cook   cup

2. When we hike we travel on _____.
foot   fold   full

3. You _____ wear strong
boots when you go hiking.
should   stood   shush

4. There are lots of trees in the _____.
would   will   woods

5. A stream is also called a _____.
buck   broke   brook

6. I _____ on the top of the
mountain.   sound   stood   soon

7. _____ at the bird in the nest!
loop   look   lose

8. There are many places we _____ like to visit.
wood   work   would

9. I will write a _____ about our adventures.
brook   brick   book

SCHOOL-HOME CONNECTION Help your child
write a list of words that rhyme with *look*.

93

Practice Book
Banner Days

▶ **Complete the sentences. On each line, write a word from the box.**

| connects | distance | features | mapmaker | peel |

1. A map tells you the _____ between two places.

2. A _____ is a person who makes maps.

3. To picture making a flat map of the round Earth,

_____ an orange. Then lay the skin flat.

4. Cities and rivers are _____ that some maps show.

5. Sometimes a line _____ two cities on a map. The line tells how far one place is from the other.

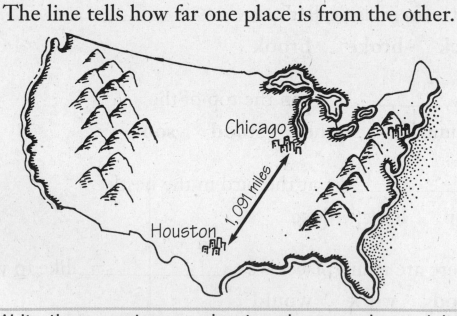

Chicago

1,091 miles

Houston

TRY THIS! Write three sentences about a place you have visited. Is it far away? Did you enjoy yourself? Use as many Vocabulary Words as possible.

© Harcourt

Name _____

Skill Reminder • The verbs *come* and *run* tell about now. Add *s* to *come* and *run* to tell what *he, she,* or *it* does.

• The verbs *came* and *ran* tell about the past.

▶ Read the words under each line. Choose the correct verb to finish the sentence. Write it on the line.

1. Most people _____ by train.
   (comes come)

2. It _____ into town at noon.
   (comes come)

3. The trains _____ on time.
   (runs run)

4. That man _____ on a bike.
   (came come)

5. Some people _____ by bus.
   (comes come)

6. The bus _____ on time.
   (runs run)

7. Long ago, the bus _____ late.
   (ran runs)

8. Sometimes people _____ for the train.
   (runs run)

95

Practice Book
Banner Days

▶ Read the words in the box. Put the words in
the box under the correct column. Write the
words in syllables.

butcher	trumpet	sandwich	basket
squirrel	children	slipper	hundred
princess	chestnut	daughter	scribble

VCCCV Words

_____

_____

_____

_____

_____

_____

VCCV Words

_____

_____

_____

_____

_____

_____

SCHOOL-HOME CONNECTION With your child,
look through a dictionary for several words with the
VCCCV or VCCV patterns. Point out the syllable marks
in the dictionary.

96

Practice Book
Banner Days

© Harcourt

Name _____

▶ **Read the Table of Contents. Then answer the questions.**

**The Best Bug Book
Table of Contents**

1. On which page would you begin to find information on feeding bugs?

- ○ page 1
- ○ page 5
- ○ page 10
- ○ page 15

> **Tip**
> Use your finger to guide you as you read.

2. Which chapter would tell you the most about big bugs?

- ○ Chapter 1
- ○ Chapter 2
- ○ Chapter 3
- ○ Chapter 4

> **Tip**
> Read each chapter title again.

© Harcourt

SCHOOL-HOME CONNECTION With your child, look at a table of contents. Have your child try to figure out what kind of information might be in the various chapters.

Practice Book
Banner Days

Name _____

▶ **Circle the best answer to each riddle.**

1. This is a word part. **preview   prefix   prepare**

2. When you tell a story
again, you do this. **review   resend   retell**

3. Do this to your shoelace. **resend   retie   retire**

4. You may do this
to your suitcase. **recheck   repack   reread**

5. Do this with library books. **return   repay   rewrite**

6. You do this when you pay ahead. **prefix   repay   prepay**

7. If your glass is empty, you
may do this. **rejoin   refold   refill**

8. If you just closed the door, you
may do this. **rework   reopen   reuse**

SCHOOL-HOME CONNECTION Review words that
have the prefixes *re-* and *pre-*. See how many other
words with those prefixes you and your child can
name.

98

Practice Book
Banner Days

© Harcourt

▶ **Finish the story. On each line, write a word from the box.**

| you | wound | through | youth | soup | group | routine |

Grandma's House

Sometimes I go to my grandmother's house. Every day that

I am there I follow the same **(1)** _____.

A **(2)** _____ of my relatives

comes over for lunch. Grandma makes a big

pot of **(3)** _____ for us

to eat. If I were to cut my finger while

slicing the vegetables, Grandma would put

a bandage on my **(4)** _____. After lunch, my

grandmother takes me to the **(5)** _____ center to

play games. We walk **(6)** _____ the woods to get

there. Next time I go, **(7)** _____ should come

with me.

© Harcourt

SCHOOL-HOME CONNECTION Help your child
make up a recipe for a crazy soup. Write down the
name of the soup and the ingredients.

99

Practice Book
Banner Days

▶ **Read the Spelling Words. Write the words where they belong.**

Words with *ou*	
1. _____	6. _____
2. _____	7. _____
3. _____	8. _____
4. _____	9. _____
5. _____	10. _____

Spelling Words

routine
through
you
soup
group
wound
coupon
youth
throughway
throughout
childhood
should
able
board
seat

▶ **Sort the words that are left by the number of syllables.**

One-Syllable Words	Two-Syllable Words
11. _____	14. _____
12. _____	15. _____
13. _____	

© Harcourt

Name _____

▶ **Solve each riddle. Write a word from the box on the line.**

group	throughway	routine	
wound	youth	throughout	soup

1. This is a path or a road that goes through

   something. It's a _____.

2. This is a hot liquid with vegetables or

   meat. It's _____.

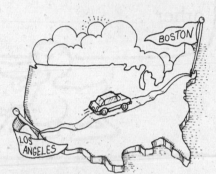

3. If you are young, you are in this.

   It's your _____.

4. If you traveled all around the country, you did this.

   You traveled _____ the United States.

5. A cut is one of these. It's a _____.

6. If you traveled with many people, you traveled in one of

   these. It's a _____.

7. If you do the same things every day, you have

   one of these. It's your _____.

SCHOOL-HOME CONNECTION Help your child make up a story about a trip he or she would like to take. Write a few sentences about the trip. Use at least two *ou* words.

101

Practice Book
Banner Days

© Harcourt

▶ **Complete the sentences. On each line, write a word from the suitcases.**

companions   sturdy   cassette   luggage   relatives

We will need to write to Grandma Duck and lots of other _____ .

Let's pack our things in our _____ .

Are these shoes _____ enough for hiking?

It's going to be a long ride, son! You may want to take your _____ player.

I'm bringing plenty of _____ to keep me company!

 TRY THIS! Write about getting ready for a trip. Use as many Vocabulary Words as you can.

© Harcourt

Name _____

Skill Reminder • The verbs *go* and *do* tell about now. When the naming part of a sentence is *he, she, it,* or a noun that names one person or thing, add *es* to *go* and *do*. • The verbs *went* and *did* tell about the past.

▶ Complete the sentences. Write a word from the box on each line.

| go | goes | went | do | does | did |

1. Subway trains _____ much faster than a person can walk.

2. A subway train _____ not have to wait in traffic.

3. Yesterday, we _____ on a subway ride.

4. We thought the driver _____ a good job.

5. You must see how fast a subway train _____.

6. What can you _____ if you miss a train?

7. Don't worry. Soon after one train _____, another train comes.

8. I am glad we _____ on a subway ride.

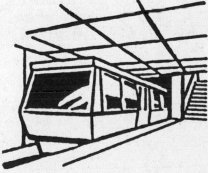

Practice Book
Banner Days

▶ **Choose the word that has the same sound as the underlined letters in the first word. Fill in the circle of the answer you choose.**

Example: y<u>ou</u>thful

     ○ train

     ○ crow

     ○ through

1 y<u>ou</u>

     ○ brook

     ○ young

     ○ soup

> 💡 **Tip**
> Say each choice aloud and listen for the same sound.

2 tr<u>ou</u>pe

     ○ throughway

     ○ trust

     ○ throw

> 💡 **Tip**
> You can ignore the choices that don't make sense.

3 thr<u>ou</u>ghout

     ○ throwing

     ○ regroup

     ○ outgrow

Name _____

▶ **Read each paragraph. Then answer the questions.**

Puerto Rico is the best place for your vacation. You will love the sunshine and our beautiful beaches. Great food and friendly people make your visit special. In the evenings, you will want to dance all night to the wonderful music in our clubs. Bring your children and have a vacation you will always remember.

1. What is the author's purpose— to entertain *or* to persuade?

_____

💡 **Tip**
Think about the words the author uses to describe Puerto Rico.

2. What does the author want you to do— come to Puerto Rico *or* take a cruise?

_____

💡 **Tip**
Reread the paragraph to check your answer

© Harcourt

SCHOOL-HOME CONNECTION With your child, look at an advertisement or newspaper article. Discuss with your child the author's purpose for writing the item.

105

Practice Book
Banner Days

Name _____

▶ Add *mis–* or *under–* to the words in the box.
Write each new word where it belongs on the
chart. Make sure the words you write make sense.

lead	place	stand	print	go
water	understand	ground	wear	spell

mis	under
1. _____	6. _____
2. _____	7. _____
3. _____	8. _____
4. _____	9. _____
5. _____	10. _____

▶ Write the word from the chart that best completes each
sentence.

11. I always _____
my keys.

12. The subway runs _____ .

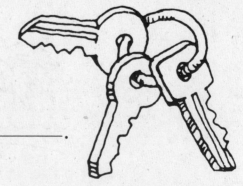

SCHOOL-HOME CONNECTION Write *mis–* and
under– on several strips of paper or on index cards.
Then write the words *lead, place, print, understand,
spell, stand, go, water, ground,* and *wear* on others. Ask your
child to match the prefix cards with the word cards to form
words from this exercise.

Practice Book
Banner Days

Name _____

▶ **Write the words from the box in the column where they belong. Read your lists to a partner.**

lawn	crawled	taught	naughty	yawn	saw
draw	seesaw	daughter		paw	law

cl**aw**

c**au**ght

_____   _____

_____   _____

_____   _____

_____

_____

_____

SCHOOL-HOME CONNECTION With your child, make up nonsense sentences using as many of the *augh* and *aw* words as possible. For example: "The naughty lawn crawled onto the seesaw." Encourage your child to play with the words.

107

© Harcourt

Name _____

▶ Read the Spelling Words. Sort the words
and write them where they belong.

**Spelling
Words**

Words with *aw*	Words With *au*
1. _____	7. _____
2. _____	8. _____
3. _____	9. _____
4. _____	10. _____
5. _____	
6. _____	

crawled
saw
caught
seesaw
draw
lawn
naughty
taught
daughter
yawn
throughout
coupon
hole
night
story

▶ Sort the words that are left by the number
of syllables.

One-Syllable Words	Two-Syllable Words
11. _____	13. _____
12. _____	14. _____
	15. _____

© Harcourt

Name _____

▶ **Write a word from the box to answer each riddle.**

lawn	crawled	taught	naughty
yawn	caught	saw	draw

1. You do this when you use a pencil to make a

picture. You _____.

2. If you spotted an island, you did this.

You _____ the island.

3. If your boat was stuck between two rocks, it was this.

Your boat was _____.

4. Before you learned to walk, you probably

did this. You _____.

5. When you get tired, you do this.

You _____.

6. If you were bad, you were this. You were _____.

7. If you learned how to sail, someone did this. Someone

_____ you.

8. This is the grassy place outside of a house. It's the

_____.

© Harcourt

SCHOOL-HOME CONNECTION Help your child make up a story about sailing. Use as many aw or augh words as you can.

109

Practice Book
Banner Days

▶ **Complete the sentences. On each line, write a word from the box.**

| cozy | drifted | fleet | launched | looming | realized |

1. On Saturday morning, Will _____ his new boat.

2. "It's not part of a _____, but it will get there just fine on its own."

3. All day, Will's boat _____ slowly along.

4. Once he had to turn the boat almost sideways when he saw

a big rock _____ in front of him.

5. By the middle of the afternoon, he _____ that he must head for home.

6. "Boats are nice, but at night a _____ house is best," he said.

 TRY THIS! Think about different ways to travel—boat, car, spaceship, skateboard. Use the Vocabulary Words to write sentences about your favorite way to travel.

© Harcourt

Name _____

Skill Reminder • **A helping verb works with the main verb to tell about an action.** *Has, have,* and *had* can be used as helping verbs.

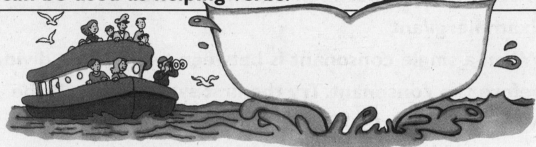

▶ **Complete the sentences. Write the helping verb *has*, *have*, or *had* on each line.**

1. I _____ not yet met the new captain.

2. The captain _____ gone on many trips.

3. _____ you ever been on a boat?

4. Mr. Wicks _____ never seen a whale.

5. He _____ gone to sea many times.

6. I _____ watched many boats sail on the water.

7. A big boat _____ just now sailed near the shore.

8. I _____ always liked sailboats the best.

TRY THIS! Write three sentences about an adventure you and your friends had in the past. Use a helping verb and a main verb in each sentence. Draw a picture to go with your sentences.

© Harcourt

Syllable Rule • **When two vowels come together in a word and have separate sounds, divide the word between the two vowels.**
Example: gi/ant

• **When a single consonant is between two vowels, divide before the consonant. Try the first syllable long. If the word makes sense, keep it!**
Example: ti/ger pa/per

• **If the word doesn't make sense, divide after the consonant and try it short.**
Example: drag/on vis/it

▶ Read the words in the box. Write each word where it belongs in the chart. Divide the words into syllables.

| silence | balance | writer | winter | madam | boa |
| neon | poet | melon | favor | shaken | trial |

ti/ger	gi/ant	vis/it
1. _____	5. _____	9. _____
2. _____	6. _____	10. _____
3. _____	7. _____	11. _____
4. _____	8. _____	12. _____

© Harcourt

Name _____

▶ **Choose the correct word to complete each sentence.**

1. Please _____ me a letter when you take your boat trip.

○ right

○ write

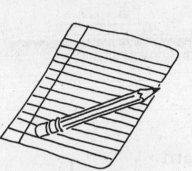

Tip
Try to picture the correct answer in your mind.

2. The mouse's home was flooded by _____.

○ rein

○ rain

Tip
Think of the most common spelling of the word. Try that first.

3. Three mice and one mole made _____ small animals on the ship.

○ four

○ for

Tip
Think about the meaning of the word in the sentence. Then choose an answer.

SCHOOL-HOME CONNECTION With your child, make a list of a few homophones. Help your child draw a picture showing the various meanings of the words.

113

Practice Book
Banner Days

© Harcourt

Name _____

Montigue on the
High Seas

Review:
Contractions
'll, n't, 's

▶ **Read the story. On each line, write the two words that make up the underlined contraction.**

(1) Isn't it fun to learn something new? I **(2)** don't know how to play the piano yet, but **(3)** I'll soon learn. My teacher is good. **(4)** She'll help me learn to play. She says that you **(5)** can't practice too much. **(6)** We'll have a recital when I am ready. I **(7)** shouldn't complain about having to practice. **(8)** It's something that all musicians must do.

1. _____

2. _____

3. _____

4. _____

5. _____

6. _____

7. _____

8. _____

SCHOOL-HOME CONNECTION Ask your child to think of a musical instrument. Have your child choose three contractions from the story and use them in new sentences about learning to play that instrument.

114

© Harcourt

▶ **Circle the answer to each riddle and write the word on the line.**

1. Something that is late is this.

override   overweight   overdue

_____

2. Someone who frowns a lot might be this.

unimportant   unfriendly   understanding

_____

3. A plane flies this way when you are below it.

overboard   overhead   overdue

_____

4. You do this to a flag before you can raise it on the pole.

unfold   unhappy   unheard

_____

5. When you pour too much water in a glass, it begins to do this.

overhead   overnight   overflow

_____

SCHOOL-HOME CONNECTION Brainstorm words with *over-* and *un-* with your child. Then have your child guess the meanings of the words and write sentences for three of the words.

115

Practice Book
Banner Days

© Harcourt

▶ **Read the Spelling Words. Sort the words and write them where they belong.**

Words with *over–*	Words with *un–*
1. _____	6. _____
2. _____	7. _____
3. _____	8. _____
4. _____	9. _____
5. _____	10. _____

Spelling Words

overdue
overnight
overboard
overflow
overhead
unfriendly
unsure
uneven
unfair
unfold
daughter
yawn
hungry
group
above

▶ **Sort the words that are left by the number of syllables.**

One-Syllable Words	Two-Syllable Words
11. _____	13. _____
12. _____	14. _____
	15. _____

© Harcourt

▶ **Finish the story. On each line, write the word from the box that completes the sentence.**

unsure	unfold	overnight	overdue	overhead

First Flight

"It's been months since I've had a chance to fly," said the

pilot. "My flight has been **(1)** _____ for a long

time. "I have to make sure to bring my sleeping bag so I can

stay **(2)** _____ when I land."

The pilot scratched his head. "My map is stuck together

and I'm **(3)** _____ of where the airport is."

Just then an airplane flew above the pilot. "What's that

noise **(4)** _____?" asked the pilot as he looked

up. "A plane!" he shouted. "Maybe that pilot can help me

(5) _____ the map."

SCHOOL-HOME CONNECTION Together with your
child, brainstorm a list of things that you can *unfold*.

117

Practice Book
Banner Days

Name _____

▶ **Finish the story. On each line, write a word
from the box.**

feat	heroine	hospitality
refused	spectators	stood

A noise startled Milly. Three young cats had fallen into the river

and were crying for help. Milly **(1)** _____ to stand
by and watch. She jumped in and pulled them out. "Milly is a

(2) _____!" all the **(3)** _____ said.
"She saved Jack and his brothers!"

Jack told the crowd about Milly's **(4)** _____.
"She saved three of us in one day. That tops a record that has

(5) _____ for years," he said. Mrs. Cat gave a party

for Milly. Milly thanked Mrs. Cat for her **(6)** _____.
"I was just helping my friends," she said.

TRY THIS! Draw a picture of someone doing a brave thing. Write four
sentences using Vocabulary Words that tell about your picture.

© Harcourt

Name _____

Skill Reminder • **A contraction is a short way to write two words. An apostrophe takes the place of the missing letter or letters.**

▶ **Read the sentences. On each line, write the two words that make up the underlined contraction.**

1. <u>I'm</u> glad my dad likes model airplanes. _____

2. Every week <u>there's</u> a new model on the kitchen table. _____

3. When I get up in the morning, I <u>can't</u> wait to see whether Dad finished building another model airplane. _____

4. When <u>it's</u> raining, I can have fun indoors. _____

5. <u>That's</u> when Dad lets me help him. _____

6. I <u>don't</u> get bored at all. _____

7. Dad thinks <u>we're</u> a good team. _____

8. He says he <u>wouldn't</u> have as much fun by himself. _____

TRY THIS! Write three sentences about something you like to do after school. See how many contractions you can use.

Practice Book
Banner Days

Syllable Rule	• **Divide a compound word between the two words:** *shoe/lace.*

• **Divide between the base word and the prefix, the suffix, or ending:** *pre/view.*

• **Divide between two consonants that fall between two vowels:** *ham/mer.*

▶ Read the words. Write each word in syllables.

1. dollar _____

2. piglet _____

3. problem _____

4. cowboy _____

5. fearful _____

6. preschool _____

7. helpless _____

8. Sunday _____

9. unfold _____

10. textbook _____

Name _____

▶ **Read the story. Then answer the questions.**

The weather was terrible. Heavy snow was falling in the city. The ground was very icy. Linda, the pilot, looked at the dark sky. This kind of weather could be very dangerous. The safety of the passengers was most important. She knew what she had to do. She could not fly the plane now.

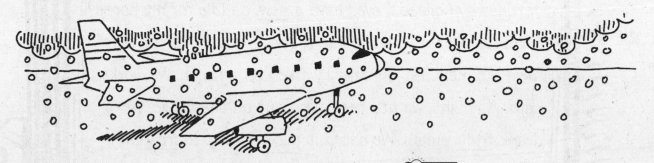

1. Which sentence would go best at the end of the paragraph?

　○　She must wait until the bad weather passed.

　○　She must clean the airplane's cockpit.

　○　She must fix the airplane's wings.

💡 **Tip**

Read the paragraph with each possible sentence at the end.

2. When the bad weather passes, the first thing Linda will probably do is

　○　get on another airplane.

　○　fly the plane.

　○　park the airplane.

💡 **Tip**

Read all the choices. Choose the one that makes the most sense.

© Harcourt

Practice Book
Banner Days

Name _____

Ruth Law Thrills
a Nation

Review:
Vowel digraphs
/ōō/ ew, ui

▶ **Read the diary entry. On each line, write the underlined word in the correct column of the chart.**

Dear Diary:

I want to be a cowboy. I want to gallop along in <u>pursuit</u> of runaway horses. I even have a <u>new</u> saddle for my horse Star. I got Star when he was a pony. He <u>grew</u> up on our farm like me. Last summer I worked on a ranch. We worked hard. At night, we ate beef <u>stew</u> out on the range. We drank <u>fruit</u> punch. We called it <u>juice</u>. I want a <u>crew</u> of cowboys to <u>recruit</u> me today!

Your pal,

Luis

ew   **ui**

1. _____   5. _____

2. _____   6. _____

3. _____   7. _____

4. _____   8. _____

Practice Book
Banner Days

© Harcourt

Skills and Strategies Index

COMPREHENSION

PHONICS/DECODING

Skills and Strategies Index

GRAMMAR

LITERARY RESPONSE AND ANALYSIS

SPELLING

VOCABULARY

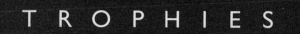

· TROPHIES ·

End-of-Selection Tests

Banner Days

The Day Jimmy's Boa Ate the Wash

Directions: For items 1–18, fill in the circle in front of the correct answer. For items 19–20, write the answer.

Vocabulary

1. The egg did not hit Maria because she _____ .
   Ⓐ sense   Ⓑ ducked
   Ⓒ suppose   Ⓓ boring

2. Dad got a new _____ for our farm.
   Ⓐ suppose   Ⓑ ducked
   Ⓒ tractor   Ⓓ boring

3. That idea makes good _____ .
   Ⓐ sense   Ⓑ boring
   Ⓒ suppose   Ⓓ haze

4. Yes, I _____ you did your best.
   Ⓐ ducked   Ⓑ suppose
   Ⓒ tractor   Ⓓ numbers

5. Most stories are exciting, but that one is _____ .
   Ⓐ ducked   Ⓑ suppose
   Ⓒ tractor   Ⓓ boring

Comprehension

6. This book is most like a _____ .
   Ⓐ poem   Ⓑ play
   Ⓒ folktale   Ⓓ fantasy

Practice Book
Banner Days

7. What words does the girl use to tell her mother about the class trip?

Ⓐ exciting and fun   Ⓑ scary and dull

Ⓒ boring and dull   Ⓓ happy and fun

8. Why does the farmer crash his tractor into the haystack?

Ⓐ He isn't paying attention to where he is going.

Ⓑ He knocks it over so the class can play in it.

Ⓒ The cow is crying.

Ⓓ He wants to say hello to the class.

9. Why is the farmer yelling at the pigs?

Ⓐ The farmer wants them off the school bus.

Ⓑ The farmer wants to feed them lunch.

Ⓒ The cow is crying.

Ⓓ The farmer's wife is angry.

10. In this story, the pigs usually eat _____ .

Ⓐ hay   Ⓑ corn on the cob

Ⓒ eggs   Ⓓ whatever they can find

11. Why do the hens start flying around when they see the boa constrictor?

Ⓐ They are saying hello to the boa.

Ⓑ They are scared of the boa.

Ⓒ The boa tries to eat one of the eggs.

Ⓓ The boa hisses at them.

12. What does the girl tell about first in the story?

Ⓐ Jimmy drops his boa constrictor in the hen house.

Ⓑ A cow starts crying.

Ⓒ An egg breaks on Jenny's head.

Ⓓ Marianne throws an egg at Jenny.

13. What starts the odd happenings at the farm?

Ⓐ the farmer's wife screaming

Ⓑ Jimmy taking his boa into the hen house

Ⓒ students leaving their lunches on the bus

Ⓓ pigs getting on the school bus

14. Who is Mrs. Stanley?

Ⓐ the farmer's wife   Ⓑ the girl's mother

Ⓒ a parent of a student   Ⓓ the teacher

15. Why does the class leave the farm in a hurry?

Ⓐ Jimmy wants to leave his boa constrictor.

Ⓑ The bus driver says that they are late.

Ⓒ Their teacher is upset that the farmer's wife is screaming.

Ⓓ The farmer tells the class to leave right away.

16. Which word best tells what the class is like?

Ⓐ wild   Ⓑ shy

Ⓒ quiet   Ⓓ brave

17. Where does the girl's story take place?

Ⓐ at the farm   Ⓑ on the school bus

Ⓒ at the girl's house   Ⓓ at the girl's school

18. Why did the writer write this story?

Ⓐ to give the reader something funny to read

Ⓑ to tell what boa constrictors are like

Ⓒ to talk about how to behave on a class trip

Ⓓ to tell what farms are like

19. Think about the story's title. Tell why the farmer's wife is screaming.

_____

_____

_____

_____

_____

20. Is this story real or make-believe? Why?

_____

_____

_____

_____

_____

Grade 2-2

© Harcourt

How I Spent My Summer Vacation

Directions: For items 1–18, fill in the circle in front of the correct answer. For items 19–20, write the answer.

Vocabulary

1. If you _____, you will feel better.
Ⓐ relax   Ⓑ imagination
Ⓒ plains   Ⓓ captured

2. The cat _____ the mouse.
Ⓐ matador   Ⓑ captured
Ⓒ plains   Ⓓ vacation

3. My family went on a trip for our summer _____.
Ⓐ imagination   Ⓑ manners
Ⓒ relax   Ⓓ vacation

4. Cowboys and cattle live on the _____.
Ⓐ matador   Ⓑ captured
Ⓒ plains   Ⓓ manners

5. The author had a great _____ to write this story.
Ⓐ vacation   Ⓑ relax
Ⓒ captured   Ⓓ imagination

6. On the class trip, everyone showed good _____.
Ⓐ matador   Ⓑ manners
Ⓒ plains   Ⓓ vacation

Grade 2-2

7. The _____ waved a red flag at the bull.

Ⓐ captured   Ⓑ imagination

Ⓒ vacation   Ⓓ matador

Comprehension

8. Wallace went to his aunt's house aboard a _____ .

Ⓐ train   Ⓑ car

Ⓒ bus   Ⓓ wagon

9. Why do Wallace's parents send him out West?

Ⓐ They want some time alone.

Ⓑ They think that he will be bored at home.

Ⓒ They are worried that his imagination is getting too wild.

Ⓓ They want his aunt to teach him to read.

10. At first, Wallace thinks that the cowboys are _____ .

Ⓐ wild and loud   Ⓑ mean and quiet

Ⓒ dirty and mean   Ⓓ shy but friendly

11. Why do the cowboys capture Wallace?

Ⓐ They are angry at his aunt.

Ⓑ They are angry at his parents.

Ⓒ One of the cowboys is sick.

Ⓓ One of the cowboys has quit.

© Harcourt

12. Think about Wallace's postcard to his aunt. How does Wallace feel about being carried off?

- Ⓐ not afraid
- Ⓑ homesick
- Ⓒ mad
- Ⓓ scared

13. Roping, riding, and making a fire with sticks are _____ .

- Ⓐ ways to get to his aunt's house
- Ⓑ things that cowboys do
- Ⓒ things that cowboys wear
- Ⓓ ways that his aunt tries to free him

14. When does Wallace get to see his aunt?

- Ⓐ the day he arrives out West
- Ⓑ the day he becomes a first-rate cowhand
- Ⓒ the day he falls off his horse
- Ⓓ the day the roundup is over

15. What terrible sight does Wallace see at his aunt's house?

- Ⓐ Aunt Fern cooking a barbecue
- Ⓑ a bull fight
- Ⓒ cowhands dancing
- Ⓓ cattle ready to stampede

16. The cattle charge at Wallace. In this story, <u>charge</u> means to _____ .

- Ⓐ pay for later
- Ⓑ rush toward
- Ⓒ blame someone
- Ⓓ ask the price

Grade 2-2

Practice Book
Banner Days

Grade 2-2

17. What does Wallace use for his "new kind of cowboying"?

Ⓐ a tablecloth   Ⓑ fire

Ⓒ a rope   Ⓓ his vest

18. When does Wallace write about his adventures in the West?

Ⓐ in the summer   Ⓑ in the fall

Ⓒ in the winter   Ⓓ in the spring

19. How does Wallace feel about the cowboys after he gets to know them?

_____

_____

_____

_____

_____

20. Is Wallace's story real or make-believe? Tell why.

_____

_____

_____

_____

_____

© Harcourt

Dear Mr. Blueberry

Directions: For items 1–18, fill in the circle in front of the correct answer. For items 19–20, write the answer.

Vocabulary

1. I hope I do not _____ you.
Ⓐ disappoint   Ⓑ forcibly
Ⓒ information   Ⓓ details

2. Many different fish live in the _____ .
Ⓐ details   Ⓑ stroke
Ⓒ meadows   Ⓓ oceans

3. I can find a lot of _____ about birds in this book.
Ⓐ disappoint   Ⓑ oceans
Ⓒ information   Ⓓ vacation

4. The author added many _____ to the story.
Ⓐ details   Ⓑ disappoint
Ⓒ information   Ⓓ stroke

5. My cat likes it when you _____ his back.
Ⓐ stroke   Ⓑ details
Ⓒ disappoint   Ⓓ forcibly

6. The farmer had to _____ put the pig in its pen.
Ⓐ details   Ⓑ information
Ⓒ disappoint   Ⓓ forcibly

Comprehension

7. "Dear Mr. Blueberry" has many _____ .

Ⓐ letters   Ⓑ poems

Ⓒ plays   Ⓓ jokes

8. You know Emily lives in Nantucket, Massachusetts because _____ .

Ⓐ she tells Mr. Blueberry where she lives

Ⓑ Mr. Blueberry likes Nantucket

Ⓒ all whales live near Nantucket

Ⓓ of the postmarks on her letters

9. Who is Mr. Blueberry?

Ⓐ a friend   Ⓑ an uncle

Ⓒ a neighbor   Ⓓ a teacher

10. What is the first thing that Emily does to help her whale?

Ⓐ She feeds him breakfast.

Ⓑ She puts salt in the pond.

Ⓒ She strokes his head.

Ⓓ She tries to make her pond bigger.

11. What is Mr. Blueberry's second reason Arthur cannot be a whale?

Ⓐ Whales never get lost.

Ⓑ Whales do not go near people.

Ⓒ Whales are too big for ponds.

Ⓓ Whales never leave oceans.

© Harcourt

12. How does Emily feel when Arthur jumps up and spurts water?
Ⓐ scared   Ⓑ happy
Ⓒ surprised   Ⓓ nervous

13. When does Arthur let Emily stroke his head?
Ⓐ when she takes him breakfast
Ⓑ after she names him Arthur
Ⓒ the day she puts salt in the pond
Ⓓ after she reads Mr. Blueberry's letter to him

14. When Mr. Blueberry writes that "whales are migratory," he means whales _____ .
Ⓐ stay in one place
Ⓑ cannot travel far
Ⓒ travel very far every day
Ⓓ travel every once in a while

15. Mr. Blueberry knows a lot about _____ .
Ⓐ whales   Ⓑ ponds
Ⓒ Emily's pond   Ⓓ Emily's parents

16. Emily thinks that Arthur left the pond because _____ .
Ⓐ the water was too hot
Ⓑ he was hungry
Ⓒ Mr. Blueberry took him away
Ⓓ Mr. Blueberry's letter made him migrate

17. How does Mr. Blueberry try to make Emily feel better after Arthur leaves?

Ⓐ He says that she can help whales when she gets older.

Ⓑ He tells her that Arthur isn't real anyway.

Ⓒ He offers to help her find Arthur.

Ⓓ He tells her that Arthur will probably come back.

18. Why is Emily sure that the whale at the beach is Arthur?

Ⓐ He smiles at her.　　Ⓑ He eats a sandwich.

Ⓒ She strokes his head.　　Ⓓ He waves good-bye.

19. Name two things that Emily feeds Arthur.

_____

_____

_____

_____

20. List two facts about blue whales that are in the story.

_____

_____

_____

_____

Cool Ali

Directions: For items 1–18, fill in the circle in front of the correct answer. For items 19–20, write the answer.

Vocabulary

1. Jane _____ the pretty red bike.
  Ⓐ mimicked   Ⓑ admired
  Ⓒ fussed   Ⓓ played

2. We did not _____ that Tom had left the room.
  Ⓐ pale   Ⓑ haze
  Ⓒ notice   Ⓓ twitch

3. The baby _____ because he wanted to eat.
  Ⓐ admired   Ⓑ mimicked
  Ⓒ notice   Ⓓ fussed

4. Bob mixed white paint and red paint to make a _____ pink.
  Ⓐ haze   Ⓑ notice
  Ⓒ pale   Ⓓ mimicked

5. The children _____ the ducks when they said, "Quack, quack."
  Ⓐ fussed   Ⓑ mimicked
  Ⓒ haze   Ⓓ pale

6. We could not see the sun because of the _____ .
  Ⓐ notice   Ⓑ pale
  Ⓒ admired   Ⓓ haze

Practice Book
Banner Days

Grade 2-2

Comprehension

7. "Cool Ali" is most like a _____ .
  (A) nonfiction book   (B) science book
  (C) real story   (D) folktale

8. What does Ali like to do?
  (A) draw   (B) sing
  (C) dance   (D) play

9. Why does Ali go outside?
  (A) She wants to talk with Mrs. Frye.
  (B) She needs to buy some sidewalk chalk.
  (C) It is too hot to stay indoors.
  (D) She wants to play with Ira.

10. When Ali goes outdoors, what is everyone thinking about?
  (A) the heat   (B) the coming storm
  (C) the fussing babies   (D) the cool breeze

11. How does Mrs. Frye show that she likes Ali's drawing?
  (A) Mrs. Frye takes off her sandals and wiggles her toes in the pretend water.
  (B) Mrs. Frye makes a newspaper fan for Ali.
  (C) Mrs. Frye smiles and says thank you.
  (D) Mrs. Frye splashes the pretend water on her face.

© Harcourt

12. What does Ali draw to keep Ira cool?

    Ⓐ the North Wind   Ⓑ a lake

    Ⓒ a beach umbrella   Ⓓ a fan

13. Where does the story take place?

    Ⓐ on a farm   Ⓑ in a city

    Ⓒ at a beach   Ⓓ near the North Pole

14. What does Mr. Boyle do after Ali draws the North Wind?

    Ⓐ complains there is too much wind

    Ⓑ looks for the polar bear

    Ⓒ puts his feet in Mrs. Frye's lake

    Ⓓ pretends he is cold and makes his teeth chatter

15. Ali makes everyone feel cooler by drawing _____ .

    Ⓐ a snowstorm   Ⓑ rain drops

    Ⓒ polka dots   Ⓓ a polar bear

16. No one notices the rain because everyone _____ .

    Ⓐ is too hot

    Ⓑ is playing with the babies

    Ⓒ is busy enjoying the snow

    Ⓓ has gone inside the building

Grade 2-2

Practice Book
Banner Days

17. Pinged, drummed, and hissed are sounds
that _____ .

Ⓐ a band makes   Ⓑ chalk makes

Ⓒ hot weather makes   Ⓓ rain makes

18. "Oh, no," Ali moaned. "Oh, no!" In this story,
moaned means _____ .

Ⓐ washed away

Ⓑ made a low, sad sound

Ⓒ cheered loudly

Ⓓ said something over and over

19. What gives Ali the idea to draw a raging blizzard?

_____

_____

_____

_____

20. How does Ali feel about the rain? Why?

_____

_____

_____

_____

_____

The Emperor's Egg

Directions: For items 1–18, fill in the circle in front of the correct answer. For items 19–20, write the answer.

Vocabulary

1. The ducks _____ up to the children to get something to eat.
   Ⓐ hatch   Ⓑ waddled
   Ⓒ miserable   Ⓓ wanted

2. We are sad and _____ because our cat is lost.
   Ⓐ slippery   Ⓑ hatch
   Ⓒ waddled   Ⓓ miserable

3. A hen sits on her eggs until they _____ .
   Ⓐ hatch   Ⓑ horizon
   Ⓒ miserable   Ⓓ waddled

4. I saw the sun appear on the _____ .
   Ⓐ waddled   Ⓑ slippery
   Ⓒ horizon   Ⓓ miserable

5. The ice on the pond is cold and _____ .
   Ⓐ flippers   Ⓑ slippery
   Ⓒ waddled   Ⓓ horizon

6. A penguin does not have hands, but it has _____ .
   Ⓐ flippers   Ⓑ slippery
   Ⓒ hatch   Ⓓ horizon

© Harcourt

Grade 2-2

Practice Book
Banner Days

Comprehension

7. In this book, Antarctica is called a big _____ .
Ⓐ meadow   Ⓑ lake
Ⓒ island   Ⓓ jungle

8. In this book, who lives on Antarctica?
Ⓐ many children   Ⓑ penguins
Ⓒ ducks   Ⓓ no one

9. In summer, the weather on Antarctica is _____ .
Ⓐ hot and sunny   Ⓑ cold and windy
Ⓒ rainy and hot   Ⓓ really nice

10. _____ penguin takes care of the Emperor penguin egg.
Ⓐ Granddaughter   Ⓑ Baby
Ⓒ Father   Ⓓ Mother

11. The female penguin is _____ than the male penguin.
Ⓐ smaller   Ⓑ sadder
Ⓒ bigger   Ⓓ tamer

12. The female penguin spends the winter _____ .
Ⓐ finding food for her baby
Ⓑ protecting her egg
Ⓒ swimming in the ocean
Ⓓ getting food for the male penguin

13. A father penguin keeps the egg warm by _____ .
- Ⓐ sitting on it
- Ⓑ putting the egg under its tummy
- Ⓒ putting it on the snow and ice
- Ⓓ putting it under the mother's tummy

14. How long does it take a penguin egg to hatch?
- Ⓐ two days
- Ⓑ two weeks
- Ⓒ two months
- Ⓓ two summers

15. Winter in Antarctica begins in _____ .
- Ⓐ December
- Ⓑ March
- Ⓒ July
- Ⓓ May

16. Penguins have _____ to help them keep warm.
- Ⓐ no fat under their skin
- Ⓑ feathers and fur
- Ⓒ lots of fat under their skin
- Ⓓ a big fur coat

17. A baby penguin is called a _____ .
- Ⓐ hen
- Ⓑ pup
- Ⓒ child
- Ⓓ chick

18. Every adult penguin has its own special _____ .
- Ⓐ call
- Ⓑ fingerprint
- Ⓒ nose
- Ⓓ whistle

Practice Book
Banner Days

19. Name two things a father penguin does to care for a baby penguin.

_____

_____

_____

_____

_____

_____

_____

20. How does a father penguin get food for his baby?

_____

_____

_____

_____

_____

_____

_____

The Pine Park Mystery

Directions: For items 1–18, fill in the circle in front of the correct answer. For items 19–20, write the answer.

Vocabulary

1. Today is a _____ day because nothing special is going on.
Ⓐ caused   Ⓑ removes
Ⓒ typical   Ⓓ cornered

2. Close the _____ on your bracelet.
Ⓐ removes   Ⓑ typical
Ⓒ caused   Ⓓ clasp

3. The directions were so long we were _____ .
Ⓐ confused   Ⓑ objects
Ⓒ typical   Ⓓ caused

4. We have many _____ in the box.
Ⓐ removes   Ⓑ objects
Ⓒ typical   Ⓓ confused

5. Jill _____ her boots before she comes into the house.
Ⓐ objects   Ⓑ caused
Ⓒ removes   Ⓓ typical

6. The rain _____ the drawing to be washed away.
Ⓐ cornered   Ⓑ caused
Ⓒ confused   Ⓓ removes

Practice Book
Banner Days

7. It looked as if the cat _____ the mouse, but the mouse got away.

(A) cornered   (B) typical

(C) objects   (D) caused

Comprehension

8. When does this play take place?

(A) in the future   (B) long ago

(C) in the present   (D) in the winter

9. Where does this play take place?

(A) in front of a bookstore

(B) on a farm

(C) on a school playground

(D) in a town park

10. Who jogs in place?

(A) Mayor Pitt   (B) Coach Lee

(C) Jeff   (D) Chief Wilson

11. Why is Lan bored before she loses her bracelet?

(A) The weather is bad.

(B) She is not getting along with Jeff.

(C) There is nothing interesting to do.

(D) She doesn't feel well.

12. When does Chief Wilson realize his badge is missing?
- Ⓐ after he wakes up from his nap
- Ⓑ as he is talking to Miss Rosa
- Ⓒ when he goes back to the police station
- Ⓓ before he takes his nap

13. All the missing objects are listed on the sign except for the _____ .
- Ⓐ charm bracelet
- Ⓑ police badge
- Ⓒ silver pin
- Ⓓ whistle

14. Which is most important to Lan?
- Ⓐ losing her bracelet
- Ⓑ solving a mystery
- Ⓒ finding a bicycle key
- Ⓓ playing catch with Jeff

15. How are all the missing objects alike?
- Ⓐ They are pieces of jewelry.
- Ⓑ They are small and shiny.
- Ⓒ Some are round and gold.
- Ⓓ They are large and brown.

16. The runners crossing the stage obscured the key. In this play, <u>obscured</u> means _____ .
- Ⓐ ran
- Ⓑ found
- Ⓒ hid
- Ⓓ lost

Grade 2-2

17. When Chief Wilson says that the "thief isn't any*body*," he means that _____ .

   Ⓐ the thief is not a person

   Ⓑ the thief is more than one person

   Ⓒ there is no thief

   Ⓓ the thief is a famous person

18. The mynah bird has put all the stolen objects in _____ .

   Ⓐ her cage   Ⓑ the bookstore

   Ⓒ a pond   Ⓓ a tree

19. In Scene One, what is Miss Rosa looking for?

_____

_____

_____

_____

_____

20. Why does Lan want to go to the park again?

_____

_____

_____

_____

Good-bye, Curtis

Directions: For items 1–18, fill in the circle in front of the correct answer. For items 19–20, write the answer.

Vocabulary

1. Will you _____ the milk for me?
  Ⓐ grown   Ⓑ honor
  Ⓒ pour   Ⓓ route

2. Tell me the best _____ to the lake.
  Ⓐ route   Ⓑ pour
  Ⓒ clerk   Ⓓ grown

3. At the store, the _____ helped me find things.
  Ⓐ addresses   Ⓑ clerk
  Ⓒ honor   Ⓓ route

4. The little seeds have _____ into a big tree.
  Ⓐ grown   Ⓑ addresses
  Ⓒ pour   Ⓓ honor

5. Write the _____ of the club members in the book.
  Ⓐ honor   Ⓑ route
  Ⓒ grown   Ⓓ addresses

6. It is an _____ to meet the Mayor.
  Ⓐ addresses   Ⓑ honor
  Ⓒ objects   Ⓓ early

Comprehension

7. This book is most like a _____ .

Ⓐ poem   Ⓑ play

Ⓒ science book   Ⓓ story book

8. When does the story take place?

Ⓐ forty-two years ago

Ⓑ present day

Ⓒ last night

Ⓓ in the future

9. What is Curtis's job?

Ⓐ crossing guard   Ⓑ mail carrier

Ⓒ mayor   Ⓓ writer

10. People leave their gifts for Curtis _____ .

Ⓐ on their front steps

Ⓑ in his car

Ⓒ at his office

Ⓓ in their mailboxes

11. Max gives Curtis _____ .

Ⓐ a pencil sharpener

Ⓑ a small, fat book

Ⓒ candy

Ⓓ a bottle of aftershave

12. Curtis has been doing this job _____ .

    Ⓐ not very long

    Ⓑ for eight years

    Ⓒ for a long time

    Ⓓ for a year or two

13. People leave gifts for Curtis because _____ .

    Ⓐ it is his birthday

    Ⓑ he is retiring

    Ⓒ he is always on time

    Ⓓ he is going on a vacation

14. People throw a party for Curtis at _____ .

    Ⓐ his house

    Ⓑ the last house on his route

    Ⓒ his neighbor's house

    Ⓓ the first house on his route

15. People have a party for Curtis because _____ .

    Ⓐ they like him

    Ⓑ it is his birthday

    Ⓒ they want to dance and eat

    Ⓓ he just got a new job

16. After the party, Curtis dreams about _____ .

    Ⓐ his retirement   Ⓑ his vacation

    Ⓒ the party   Ⓓ people's addresses

© Harcourt

Practice Book
Banner Days

17. Which word best tells what Curtis is like?

Ⓐ lazy   Ⓑ jealous

Ⓒ sad   Ⓓ friendly

18. Writing thank-you notes is _____ .

Ⓐ thoughtful   Ⓑ brave

Ⓒ selfish   Ⓓ silly

19. Why do people share "remembering" at the party?

_____

_____

_____

_____

_____

_____

20. Why does Curtis know everyone's address by heart?

_____

_____

_____

_____

_____

_____

Max Found Two Sticks

Directions: For items 1–18, fill in the circle in front of the correct answer. For items 19–20, write the answer.

Vocabulary

1. The loud noise _____ the baby and made her cry.
  (A) appeared   (B) startled
  (C) imitated   (D) created

2. The moon _____ in the night sky.
  (A) startled   (B) imitated
  (C) created   (D) appeared

3. The _____ helped us find seats on the train.
  (A) conductor   (B) appeared
  (C) rhythm   (D) honor

4. We started to dance to the _____ of the music.
  (A) created   (B) imitated
  (C) appeared   (D) rhythm

5. We _____ a beautiful painting on the wall.
  (A) created   (B) appeared
  (C) startled   (D) conductor

6. The children _____ the cow and said, "Moo."
  (A) created   (B) startled
  (C) imitated   (D) appeared

© Harcourt

Grade 2-2

Practice Book
Banner Days

Comprehension

7. What is Max's grandpa doing?
  (A) listening to Max drum
  (B) washing the windows
  (C) sweeping the steps
  (D) raking leaves

8. Before Max starts drumming, he is _____ .
  (A) talking to his grandpa
  (B) helping his grandpa
  (C) sitting on the front steps
  (D) waiting for his mother

9. How does Max get the twigs he uses as drumsticks?
  (A) His grandpa gives them to him.
  (B) The wind knocks them down from a tree.
  (C) Max shakes a tree until they fall down.
  (D) Cindy, Shaun, and Jamal give the sticks to him.

10. Before Max drums on the cleaning bucket, he drums on _____ .
  (A) hat boxes   (B) soda bottles
  (C) his thighs   (D) the steps

11. When Max answers his grandpa with a "Pat . . . pat-tat. Putter-putter . . ." he is imitating the

_____ .

Ⓐ rhythm of the rain hitting a window

Ⓑ sound of pigeons in flight

Ⓒ beat of drums in a marching band

Ⓓ church bells

12. What is Max's mom doing before she sees Max on the steps?

Ⓐ shopping for food   Ⓑ cleaning windows

Ⓒ working at home   Ⓓ shopping for hats

13. What does Max use from Cindy, Shaun, and Jamal for part of his drum set?

Ⓐ garbage cans   Ⓑ soda bottles

Ⓒ hat boxes   Ⓓ cleaning buckets

14. Which building is around the corner from Max's house?

Ⓐ a school   Ⓑ a church

Ⓒ a train station   Ⓓ a hat shop

15. What does Max's father do for a living?

Ⓐ window washer   Ⓑ plays in a band

Ⓒ train conductor   Ⓓ policeman

Grade 2-2

16. Max learns how to drum by _____ .
  Ⓐ listening to the world and copying its rhythms
  Ⓑ taking lessons from a drummer
  Ⓒ playing the rhythms that he makes up
  Ⓓ listening to drummers on the radio

17. This book is mostly like _____ .
  Ⓐ a folktale   Ⓑ a play
  Ⓒ a story book   Ⓓ nonfiction

18. Where does this story take place?
  Ⓐ in front of Max's house
  Ⓑ at the train station
  Ⓒ next to the church
  Ⓓ inside Max's home

19. How does Max answer everybody's questions?

_____

_____

_____

20. What is the only word Max says in the story?

_____

_____

_____

Anthony Reynoso: Born to Rope

Directions: For items 1–18, fill in the circle in front of the correct answer. For items 19–20, write the answer.

Vocabulary

1. We saw horses and cows at the _____ .
  Ⓐ landscape business   Ⓑ thousands
  Ⓒ dappled   Ⓓ ranch

2. We saw a black horse and a _____ one.
  Ⓐ dappled   Ⓑ ranch
  Ⓒ thousands   Ⓓ landscape business

3. The rocks have been there for _____ of years.
  Ⓐ exhibition   Ⓑ thousands
  Ⓒ ranch   Ⓓ appeared

4. Mr. Pat runs a _____ .
  Ⓐ dappled   Ⓑ grown
  Ⓒ conductor   Ⓓ landscape business

5. The children's paintings are on _____ in the school gym.
  Ⓐ thousands   Ⓑ dappled
  Ⓒ exhibition   Ⓓ appeared

Grade 2-2

Comprehension

6. This book mostly tells about _____ .
- Ⓐ getting a new baby in the family
- Ⓑ a Mexican rodeo
- Ⓒ working in a restaurant
- Ⓓ someone's life

7. Anthony is named after his _____ .
- Ⓐ cousin
- Ⓑ mother
- Ⓒ father
- Ⓓ uncle

8. Who is telling this story?
- Ⓐ Anthony's father
- Ⓑ Anthony
- Ⓒ Anthony's mother
- Ⓓ Anthony's grandfather

9. When does Anthony get his first rope?
- Ⓐ as soon as he can walk
- Ⓑ when he starts school
- Ⓒ as soon as he can stand
- Ⓓ when he turns three years old

10. The petroglyphs are carvings that _____ .
- Ⓐ are hundreds of years old
- Ⓑ are carved in the wall of a building
- Ⓒ are well known around the world
- Ⓓ tell a story Anthony understands

© Harcourt

11. Guadalupe is always crowded at Easter because _____ .

 (A) artists come to paint the walls of buildings

 (B) a rodeo is held there

 (C) a Mission church holds a giant festival

 (D) the Yaqui Indians have ceremonies in town

12. What kind of food does Casa Reynoso serve?

 (A) Italian food   (B) Yaqui Indian food

 (C) Mexican food   (D) rodeo food

13. At his grandparents' ranch, Anthony does everything but _____ .

 (A) practice roping on horseback

 (B) celebrate his cousins' birthdays

 (C) play basketball

 (D) pose for family photos

14. What kind of student is Anthony?

 (A) He works hard at school.

 (B) He sometimes finishes his homework.

 (C) School is not important to him.

 (D) He likes only sports at school.

15. In Mexico, "the most famous charros are like sports stars here." <u>Charros</u> are _____ .

 (A) cowboys   (B) basketball players

 (C) rodeos   (D) teams of cowboys

16. How does Anthony feel about doing rope tricks?

Ⓐ It's too much work.

Ⓑ He's proud to work with his father.

Ⓒ He brags about it at school.

Ⓓ He'd rather play basketball.

17. At birthday parties, there is always a _____ .

Ⓐ clown   Ⓑ rodeo

Ⓒ piñata   Ⓓ charro

18. When does Anthony feel like a celebrity?

Ⓐ when he spins the rope with his teeth

Ⓑ when he performs in a show

Ⓒ when his mother watches him perform

Ⓓ when he poses for pictures with tourists

19. What does Anthony's father do on weekdays?

_____

_____

_____

20. How does Anthony feel about having a baby brother or sister?

_____

_____

_____

Chinatown

Directions: For items 1–18, fill in the circle in front of the correct answer. For items 19–20, write the answer.

Vocabulary

1. We need to buy milk when we go to the _____ .
  Ⓐ develop   Ⓑ furious
  Ⓒ grocery store   Ⓓ graceful

2. We have many _____ during the year.
  Ⓐ celebrations   Ⓑ furious
  Ⓒ graceful   Ⓓ dappled

3. The man was _____ when the dog ate his lunch.
  Ⓐ develop   Ⓑ furious
  Ⓒ ranch   Ⓓ celebrations

4. The _____ have homework every night.
  Ⓐ students   Ⓑ grocery store
  Ⓒ develop   Ⓓ appeared

5. The dancers are _____ when they dance.
  Ⓐ celebrations   Ⓑ develop
  Ⓒ sideways   Ⓓ graceful

6. With practice you will _____ into a good ball player.
  Ⓐ graceful   Ⓑ develop
  Ⓒ furious   Ⓓ honor

© Harcourt

Grade 2-2

Comprehension

7. The child in the story lives with everyone **except** a
    _____ .
    (A) mother   (B) father
    (C) grandfather   (D) grandmother

8. Who is telling this story?
    (A) Grandma   (B) Mr. Wong
    (C) Mr. Chung   (D) the child

9. How does the storyteller feel about his hometown?
    (A) furious   (B) bored
    (C) proud   (D) cornered

10. In this story a cobbler is the one who fixes _____ .
    (A) shoes   (B) crabs
    (C) feet   (D) handcarts

11. Who goes to the tai chi class?
    (A) graceful dancers
    (B) young and old students
    (C) children under 10
    (D) Grandma

12. Why does Grandma make medicinal soup?
    (A) Mother and Dad want some for lunch.
    (B) Grandma and the child are sick.
    (C) She thinks it will keep her strength up.
    (D) It is time to eat.

Practice Book
Banner Days

13. At the outdoor market, the child can barely move because _____ .
Ⓐ Grandma needs his help
Ⓑ Grandma is ready to eat
Ⓒ it is very crowded
Ⓓ Grandma will eat all the crabs

14. The child takes kung fu lessons to _____ .
Ⓐ play on Saturday
Ⓑ learn a new dance
Ⓒ develop body and mind
Ⓓ learn how to cook

15. What does the child plan to do on New Year's Day next year?
Ⓐ dance with the lion
Ⓑ march with the older kids
Ⓒ watch a tai chi exhibition
Ⓓ beat the drums

16. A <u>wok</u> is _____ .
Ⓐ hot, sizzling oil   Ⓑ a pan for cooking
Ⓒ fresh seafood   Ⓓ a noisy restaurant

17. In this book, "Gung hay fat choy" means _____ .
Ⓐ here comes the lion
Ⓑ time for the celebration
Ⓒ Happy New Year
Ⓓ let's watch the lion dance

Practice Book
Banner Days

18. This story takes place in _____ .

    Ⓐ a restaurant

    Ⓑ the park

    Ⓒ a market

    Ⓓ Chinatown

19. What does the child do to show he cares a lot for Grandma?

_____

_____

_____

_____

_____

_____

20. Name two places the child and Grandma pass on their morning walk.

_____

_____

_____

_____

_____

Directions: For items 1–18, fill in the circle in front of the correct answer. For items 19–20, write the answer.

Vocabulary

1. A _____ of birds flew over the trees.
   - Ⓐ soared
   - Ⓑ flock
   - Ⓒ glide
   - Ⓓ harbor

2. Five big ships are in the _____ .
   - Ⓐ flock
   - Ⓑ glide
   - Ⓒ harbor
   - Ⓓ develop

3. The kite _____ over our heads like a bird.
   - Ⓐ soared
   - Ⓑ harbor
   - Ⓒ glide
   - Ⓓ furious

4. The pretty boats _____ across the water.
   - Ⓐ harbor
   - Ⓑ flock
   - Ⓒ glide
   - Ⓓ swooping

5. The bird came _____ down from its nest.
   - Ⓐ swooping
   - Ⓑ flock
   - Ⓒ soared
   - Ⓓ glide

Comprehension

6. "Abuela" is most like a _____ .
   - Ⓐ fantasy
   - Ⓑ nonfiction book
   - Ⓒ poem
   - Ⓓ play

7. Abuela is my mother's mother. She is my _____ .

   Ⓐ aunt   Ⓑ neighbor

   Ⓒ grandmother   Ⓓ friend

8. Who is telling this story?

   Ⓐ a bird   Ⓑ Abuela

   Ⓒ a young girl   Ⓓ Rosalba's father

9. When Abuela and Rosalba say <u>buenos días</u>, they are saying _____ .

   Ⓐ good morning

   Ⓑ I hear you

   Ⓒ it is hot

   Ⓓ goodnight

10. Abuela and Rosalba wave at people waiting for the bus. Then what do they do?

   Ⓐ circle around the Statue of Liberty

   Ⓑ race with sailboats

   Ⓒ take a short ride to the airport

   Ⓓ visit cousin Daniel

11. When Abuela and Rosalba "glide close to the sea," they are _____ .

   Ⓐ flying smoothly and easily

   Ⓑ flying slowly

   Ⓒ being blown by the wind

   Ⓓ riding in a plane

12. What does Abuela's skirt become when she races the boats?

Ⓐ a motor   Ⓑ the wind

Ⓒ a sail   Ⓓ wings

13. Which fruits have Spanish names?

Ⓐ papaya, banana, apple

Ⓑ banana, plum, mango

Ⓒ strawberry, grape, papaya

Ⓓ papaya, banana, mango

14. Abuela first came to America by _____ .

Ⓐ ship   Ⓑ plane

Ⓒ train   Ⓓ bus

15. Rosalba thinks her uncle and aunt would be surprised because _____ .

Ⓐ Rosalba and Abuela are flying

Ⓑ Rosalba wants lemonade

Ⓒ Abuela saw her cousin

Ⓓ Abuela raced the sailboats

16. What do the clouds look like to Rosalba?

Ⓐ an airplane, a balloon, and a tree

Ⓑ a cat, a bear, and a chair

Ⓒ snow, a bear, and a bed

Ⓓ an airplane, a balloon, and a bird

17. Rosalba's father works _____ .
    Ⓐ in a park   Ⓑ on the docks
    Ⓒ in a tall building   Ⓓ at the airport

18. Which sentence is true about Abuela?
    Ⓐ Abuela is afraid of flying.
    Ⓑ Abuela loves fun and adventure.
    Ⓒ Abuela has lived in America all her life.
    Ⓓ Abuela only speaks English to Rosalba.

19. Why is the Statue of Liberty important to Abuela?

_____

_____

_____

_____

_____

20. Do Abuela and Rosalba really fly or does Rosalba imagine it?

_____

_____

_____

_____

_____

Practice Book
Banner Days

Beginner's World Atlas

Directions: For items 1–18, fill in the circle in front of the correct answer. For items 19–20, write the answer.

Vocabulary

1. I will _____ the orange for you.
Ⓐ distance ⒷＢ connects
Ⓒ peel Ⓓ features

2. The _____ draws symbols on the maps.
Ⓐ features Ⓑ distance
Ⓒ connects Ⓓ mapmaker

3. Grandma's house is a long _____ away.
Ⓐ distance Ⓑ connects
Ⓒ mapmaker Ⓓ peel

4. The branch _____ the trunk to the leaves of the tree.
Ⓐ peel Ⓑ features
Ⓒ connects Ⓓ distance

5. A physical map key shows the _____ on the map.
Ⓐ mapmaker Ⓑ distance
Ⓒ connects Ⓓ features

Grade 2-2

Grade 2-2

Comprehension

6. A _____ tells where north is on a map.
 Ⓐ map key   Ⓑ scale
 Ⓒ globe   Ⓓ compass

7. A map shows _____ .
 Ⓐ how to get somewhere
 Ⓑ why the world is flat
 Ⓒ a bird flying
 Ⓓ how to name an ocean

8. From space, you can see _____ .
 Ⓐ that the Earth is flat
 Ⓑ all the planets at one time
 Ⓒ all the Earth at one time
 Ⓓ half the Earth at one time

9. Mapmakers draw the Equator on a map to _____ .
 Ⓐ add more lines for the globe
 Ⓑ divide the Earth into North and South
 Ⓒ divide the Earth into East and West
 Ⓓ show the land and the seas

10. To understand the features on a map, use the _____ .
 Ⓐ Equator   Ⓑ map key
 Ⓒ globe   Ⓓ map scale

11. How are an ocean and a lake different?

- Ⓐ A lake is smaller than an ocean.
- Ⓑ One is water, and one is land.
- Ⓒ An ocean is surrounded by land.
- Ⓓ A lake is bigger than an ocean.

12. The largest island in the world is _____ .

- Ⓐ Greenland
- Ⓑ a peninsula
- Ⓒ Europe
- Ⓓ a forest

13. A large stream of water is a _____ .

- Ⓐ desert
- Ⓑ forest
- Ⓒ river
- Ⓓ pond

14. The author says the shape of North America is _____ .

- Ⓐ like a triangle
- Ⓑ like a square
- Ⓒ like a circle
- Ⓓ an ice cap

15. Central America _____ .

- Ⓐ is in the Sierra Nevada Mountains
- Ⓑ connects North America and South America
- Ⓒ crosses the Rocky Mountains
- Ⓓ is on the Equator

16. The largest city in North America is _____ .

- Ⓐ New York City
- Ⓑ Canada
- Ⓒ Mexico City
- Ⓓ Los Angeles

Grade 2-2

17. A shortcut between the Atlantic and Pacific Oceans is _____ .

  Ⓐ down the Nile river   Ⓑ up the Mississippi
  Ⓒ the Panama Canal   Ⓓ across Mexico

18. Ice caps can be found in _____ .

  Ⓐ South America   Ⓑ the Pacific Ocean
  Ⓒ the Caribbean Sea   Ⓓ Antarctica

19. On which continent do you live?

_____

_____

_____

_____

_____

_____

20. Is this book fiction or nonfiction? Tell why.

_____

_____

_____

_____

_____

© Harcourt

Practice Book
Banner Days

Dinosaurs Travel

Directions: For items 1–18, fill in the circle in front of the correct answer. For items 19–20, write the answer.

Vocabulary

1. We need a strong, _____ table to work on.
- Ⓐ relatives
- Ⓑ companions
- Ⓒ sturdy
- Ⓓ celebrations

2. A trip is more fun when you have _____ with you.
- Ⓐ companions
- Ⓑ cassette
- Ⓒ sturdy
- Ⓓ features

3. We can play tapes on the _____ player.
- Ⓐ cassette
- Ⓑ sturdy
- Ⓒ companions
- Ⓓ luggage

4. We saw many _____ at the party.
- Ⓐ luggage
- Ⓑ relatives
- Ⓒ sturdy
- Ⓓ protects

5. Dad put the _____ on top of the van.
- Ⓐ relatives
- Ⓑ companions
- Ⓒ luggage
- Ⓓ sturdy

Comprehension

6. What is not in the story as a way to travel?
- Ⓐ helicopter
- Ⓑ boat
- Ⓒ plane
- Ⓓ limousine

Practice Book
Banner Days

7. Books and maps can help you _____ .
Ⓐ pack luggage   Ⓑ buy a cassette
Ⓒ learn about places   Ⓓ visit relatives

8. Which item should you leave at home when you travel?
Ⓐ your toothbrush   Ⓑ shampoo
Ⓒ a map of your route   Ⓓ your pet snake

9. What is one good thing about traveling on foot?
Ⓐ You may get blisters on your feet.
Ⓑ You can see more sights.
Ⓒ You can get to places very quickly.
Ⓓ You need lots of things to help you do it.

10. If you travel by bicycle or skateboard, you _____ .
Ⓐ don't need them in good working order
Ⓑ should follow the rules of the road
Ⓒ always need to go as fast as possible
Ⓓ can make up your own rules

11. A good car game is _____ .
Ⓐ looking at different license plates
Ⓑ singing loudly
Ⓒ playing catch
Ⓓ collecting souvenirs

12. How is traveling on buses and subways alike?
Ⓐ They make a lot of stops.
Ⓑ They mostly travel underground.
Ⓒ They are always free.
Ⓓ They have tour guides on them.

13. After you hear the words *All aboard,* the _____ .
Ⓐ driver stops   Ⓑ train leaves
Ⓒ plane lands   Ⓓ train stops

14. What does a conductor do on a train?
Ⓐ drives the train
Ⓑ decides where a train will stop
Ⓒ serves food to people
Ⓓ names each stop as the train gets close to it

15. One job the ticket agent for an airline does is to _____ .
Ⓐ pick up trays after people eat
Ⓑ carry people's bags
Ⓒ sell train tickets
Ⓓ look at people's tickets

16. In this book why is security important at an airport?
Ⓐ to be sure no one brings dangerous things on the plane
Ⓑ to check that everyone has a ticket
Ⓒ to serve snacks and drinks
Ⓓ to help fly the plane

Practice Book
Banner Days

Grade 2-2

17. To help you remember your trip, you
should _____ .
(A) bring a bag (B) take pictures
(C) move your feet (D) stretch your legs

18. Which kind of travel do the words <u>take</u> <u>off</u>, <u>fasten</u>
<u>seat</u> <u>belt</u>, and <u>land</u> tell about?
(A) boat (B) train
(C) plane (D) subway

19. What does the author say may happen when you
leave your home?

_____

_____

_____

_____

_____

20. List two things that are good about getting home
from a trip.

_____

_____

_____

_____

© Harcourt

Directions: For items 1–18, fill in the circle in front of the correct answer. For items 19–20, write the answer.

Vocabulary

1. The little boat _____ on the water.
  Ⓐ fleet   Ⓑ cozy
  Ⓒ drifted   Ⓓ realized

2. Our home is warm and _____ .
  Ⓐ cozy   Ⓑ drifted
  Ⓒ looming   Ⓓ fleet

3. The _____ of ships sailed into the harbor.
  Ⓐ launched Ⓑ fleet
  Ⓒ looming   Ⓓ cozy

4. When the sun went down, we _____ we would not be home before dark.
  Ⓐ launched Ⓑ drifted
  Ⓒ realized   Ⓓ looming

5. The new ship was _____ at the celebration.
  Ⓐ realized   Ⓑ drifted
  Ⓒ cozy   Ⓓ launched

6. A big cat was _____ over the mouse.
  Ⓐ drifted   Ⓑ looming
  Ⓒ realized   Ⓓ fleet

© Harcourt

Practice Book
Banner Days

Comprehension

7. This story is most like a fantasy because the story _____ .

   Ⓐ could not happen in the real world

   Ⓑ happened a long time ago

   Ⓒ has no author

   Ⓓ does not teach a lesson

8. In this story, coming down in buckets means _____ .

   Ⓐ pails are falling from the sky

   Ⓑ it is raining very hard

   Ⓒ the buckets are full of water

   Ⓓ the animals all fell into a bucket

9. Montigue leaves his first home because _____ .

   Ⓐ it is too cold   Ⓑ the sea floods it

   Ⓒ he is very lonely   Ⓓ the rain floods it

10. Montigue is tired when he finds a bottle to sleep in because he _____ .

   Ⓐ has been walking for days

   Ⓑ has moved his belongings into his new home

   Ⓒ has been swimming for a very long time

   Ⓓ has been visiting mouse friends

11. What is the dark shadow under Montigue's bottle?

   Ⓐ an octopus   Ⓑ a passing fish

   Ⓒ a seahorse   Ⓓ a humpback whale

12. What happens first in this story?
- Ⓐ Montigue falls out of a fish's mouth.
- Ⓑ A whale throws Montigue into the air.
- Ⓒ Montigue's bottle lands on the deck of a ship.
- Ⓓ A cat chases Montigue.

13. Why do the mice think Montigue is "funny-looking"?
- Ⓐ Montigue has big ears.
- Ⓑ They don't know Montigue is a mole.
- Ⓒ Montigue is very tall for a mouse.
- Ⓓ Montigue has lost his tail at sea.

14. What are the mice most afraid of?
- Ⓐ Barnacles
- Ⓑ the sailors
- Ⓒ whales
- Ⓓ mousetraps

15. What happens after Montigue tells the mice about his adventures?
- Ⓐ Barnacles surprises them all.
- Ⓑ The mice elect him their leader.
- Ⓒ The mice cheer.
- Ⓓ Montigue takes a nap.

16. How do Montigue's adventures help the mice?
- Ⓐ They make a fleet and sail away.
- Ⓑ They discover a way to tie up Barnacles.
- Ⓒ They find a way to take over the ship.
- Ⓓ They break all the mousetraps.

Practice Book
Banner Days

17. "Montigue scuttled into a hole," and "the mice scurried in every direction, collecting supplies." In this story, <u>scuttled</u> and <u>scurried</u> tell about ways _____ .

  Ⓐ animals move quickly

  Ⓑ to sink a ship

  Ⓒ sailors get around a ship

  Ⓓ sailors catch fish

18. How is Montigue's home at the end of the story different from his first home?

  Ⓐ It is warm in the afternoon.

  Ⓑ He has lots of friendly neighbors.

  Ⓒ It is cool in the evenings.

  Ⓓ It is far from the sea.

19. What kind of bottle does Montigue climb into?

_____

_____

_____

20. How does Montigue feel about being captain of the fleet?

_____

_____

_____

Ruth Law Thrills a Nation

Directions: For items 1–18, fill in the circle in front of the correct answer. For items 19–20, write the answer.

Vocabulary

1. A crowd of _____ watched the games.
  Ⓐ refused   Ⓑ hospitality
  Ⓒ spectators   Ⓓ heroine

2. My brother _____ to let me use his ball and bat.
  Ⓐ refused   Ⓑ spectators
  Ⓒ hospitality   Ⓓ sturdy

3. In the play, the _____ saves the relatives from harm.
  Ⓐ stood   Ⓑ refused
  Ⓒ heroine   Ⓓ looming

4. We _____ in the line a long time.
  Ⓐ spectators   Ⓑ stood
  Ⓒ refused   Ⓓ hospitality

5. Winning that long a race is a great _____ .
  Ⓐ hospitality   Ⓑ refused
  Ⓒ stood   Ⓓ feat

6. The stranger was thankful for the _____ .
  Ⓐ feat   Ⓑ stood
  Ⓒ refused   Ⓓ hospitality

Grade 2-2

Comprehension

7. What did Ruth Law try to be the first to do?

   Ⓐ fly a plane without extra gas

   Ⓑ fly from New York City in a bigger plane

   Ⓒ fly from Chicago to New York City in one day

   Ⓓ fly to Chicago before nightfall

8. Why didn't Ruth feel cold on the morning of her flight?

   Ⓐ She was too excited about her flight.

   Ⓑ She had slept in four suits and a skirt.

   Ⓒ It was a very warm morning.

   Ⓓ She had slept in a tent on a hotel roof.

9. Lake Michigan is near _____ .

   Ⓐ New York City   Ⓑ Hornell, New York

   Ⓒ Chicago   Ⓓ Binghamton, New York

10. What was Ruth's "baby machine" like?

   Ⓐ Her plane was the biggest and newest kind.

   Ⓑ Her plane was tiny and old.

   Ⓒ Her plane was built for long flights.

   Ⓓ Her plane was built to carry heavy loads.

11. Which word best tells what Ruth's take-off was like?

   Ⓐ fast   Ⓑ rough

   Ⓒ graceful   Ⓓ easy

12. To prepare the plane for Ruth's flight, mechanics _____ .

Ⓐ added five gas tanks

Ⓑ removed the lights

Ⓒ attached a special roof

Ⓓ attached a special map holder

13. Why did Ruth run out of gas before she landed in Hornell?

Ⓐ The wind didn't help push her along.

Ⓑ The wind was blowing her plane sideways.

Ⓒ She flew through a bad rainstorm.

Ⓓ She hadn't known how far Hornell was.

14. Which event happened first?

Ⓐ Ruth landed near Binghamton, New York.

Ⓑ Ruth's plane came down near Hornell, New York.

Ⓒ Ruth set an American record for flying.

Ⓓ Ruth's plane arrived in New York City.

15. Why did Ruth accept the "hospitality of strangers" outside of Binghamton?

Ⓐ Her friends did not meet her.

Ⓑ She landed there because it was getting dark.

Ⓒ Her plane got caught in a tree.

Ⓓ She was hungry and tired, so she landed there.

16. When did Ruth Law make this flight?

    Ⓐ 1916   Ⓑ 1924

    Ⓒ 1935   Ⓓ 1950

17. The book tells about someone who lived _____ .

    Ⓐ ten years ago   Ⓑ in Binghamton

    Ⓒ about 90 years ago   Ⓓ in New York City

18. This book is most like a _____ .

    Ⓐ play   Ⓑ folktale

    Ⓒ fantasy   Ⓓ biography

19. Why did Ruth wear a skirt over her four suits on the way to the plane?

_____

_____

_____

_____

20. How did Ruth Law fail? How did she succeed?

_____

_____

_____

_____

_____

Grade 2-2